THE DAVIS FARMERS MARKET COOKBOOK
Tasting California's Small Farms

Georgeanne Brennan and Ann M. Evans

FOREWORD BY ALICE WATERS

Photography by Craig Lee • Styling by Ethel Brennan

MIRABELLE PRESS

To Jim, as always, who makes it all possible. —GB

For my mother, Audrey, who first taught me to cook, for my father, Ralph, and his late wife, Catherine, who introduced me to southern food, and above all for the love of my life, David, and our daughter, Hatley Rose. —AME

Text © 2012 by Georgeanne Brennan and Ann M. Evans.
Photography © 2012 by Craig Lee.
All rights reserved. No portion of this book may be reproduced or utilized in any form or by any electronic, mechanical or other means, without the prior written permission of the publisher.

ISBN 978-0-615-54113-6

Printed in the United States.
TC Printing
1215 G Street
Sacramento, CA 95814

Design by Kristine Brogno.
Art direction and photo styling by Ethel Brennan.

Photographs of UC Davis Farmers Market (lower left and lower right) by Karen Higgins/UC Davis, page 8.
Photograph of Davis Farmers Market Pavilion by Karin Higgins/UC Davis, page 21.
Photograph of Janet Wagner by John Milne/Sutter Health, page 232.
All other photographs by Craig Lee.

10 9 8 7 6 5 4 3 2 1

MIRABELLE PRESS
Davis, CA
www.davisfarmersmarketcookbook.com

Contents

Foreword by Alice Waters • 9

PART I: Introduction

Story of the Davis Farmers Market by Ann M. Evans • 14

Reflections of a Market Manager by Randii MacNear • 23

Seasonality • 24

How to Use This Book • 26

PART II: The Basics

Eight Recipes to Adapt to the Seasons • 30

Risotto • 30

Pasta • 32

Savory Gratin • 36

Savory Tart • 37

Roasted Vegetables • 40

Vegetable Fricassee • 42

Rustic Sweet Tart • 43

Fruit Pie • 45

Three Basic Stocks to Make from Scratch • 47

Vegetable Stock • 48

Chicken Stock • 48

Beef Stock • 49

PART III: The Recipes

Spring: The Season of New Growth • 55

Warm Leek Salad with Oil-Cured Olives and Eggs • 56

Deviled Eggs with Tarragon • 59

Flatbreads with Spring Onions and Feta • 60

Fava Bean Soup with Pancetta • 63

Italian Stuffed Artichokes • 64

Fresh Spring Rolls with Thai Dipping Sauce • 66

Fresh Rag Pasta with Peas and Asparagus • 69

Young Lamb with Spring Vegetables • 71

Chicken Braised in White Wine with Peas • 74

Baked Whole Cod with Ginger, Carrots, and Green Onions • 77

Baby Fingerlings with Thyme Blossoms • 79

Green Garlic Flan • 80

Old-Fashioned Apricot Pie • 83

Black Cherries in Pinot Noir Gelatin • 86

Apricot Jam • 89

Pickled Onions • 91

Vin Maison • 92

Summer: The Season of Full Growth • 95

Fried Padrón Peppers with Goat Cheese and Crostini • 96

Bruschetta with Ricotta, Dill, and Smoked Salmon • 98

Old-Fashioned Corn Chowder with Rouille • 99

Sweet Corn and Fresh Oregano Fritters • 102

Watermelon, Cucumber, and Heirloom Cherry Tomato Salad • 104

Grilled Fresh Sardines • 107

Roast Chicken with 40 Cloves of Garlic • 109

Zucchini and Gruyère Gratin • 110

Grilled Eggplant Sandwich with Grilled Sweet Peppers and Basil Aioli • 112

Planked Salmon • 115

Heirloom Tomatoes • 117

Barbecued Short Ribs with Dark Sauce • 119

Braised Okra with Tomatoes and Onion • 123

Old-Fashioned Meringues with Berries • 124

Roasted Summer Fruits with Ice Cream • 126

Plum Jam • 129

Pickled Peaches • 131

Homemade Ketchup • 133

Summer Tomato Sauce • 136

Dill Pickles • 139

Fall: The Crossover Season • 143

Grilled Persimmon Crostini with Farmer Cheese • 144

Grilled Fig and Lardon Kebabs • 146

Classic Soupe au Pistou with Fresh Shelling Beans • 149

Roasted Beet Salad with Fresh Cheese, Toasted Pistachios, and Pistachio Oil • 151

Frisée Salad with Egg and Pancetta • 152

Salad of Early Bitter Greens and Late Cherry Tomatoes • 155

Grilled Stuffed Squid • 156

Pork Country Sausage • 158

Chile Relleno Casserole with Red Sauce • 160

Creamy Grits with Collard Greens and Wild Mushrooms • 161

Roasted Lamb Shanks with Dried Fruits • 165

Musquée de Provence with New Crop Walnuts • 168

Braised Belgian Endive • 171

Persimmon Flan • 173

Sautéed Quinces, Apples, and Pears with Whipped Cream • 175

Old-Fashioned Butter Cookies with Pistachios • 176

Chutney Making • 179

Pomegranate Jelly • 181

Winter: The Dormant Season • 185

Crab Salad on Belgian Endive Leaves with Avocado • 186

Devils on Horseback • 189

Shiitake Mushroom Soup Shots • 190

Homemade Pancetta • 192

Fried Oyster Sliders with Homemade Tartar Sauce • 195

Fried Smelt with Rouille Dipping Sauce • 196

White Bean Soup with Meyer Lemon • 198

Wonton Soup with Asian Greens • 200

Radicchio Salad with Blood Oranges • 203

Tomato Aspic with Green Goddess Dressing • 204

Tempura Vegetables with Shredded Daikon Dipping Sauce • 207

Cracked Dungeness Crab • 211

Savoy Cabbage Rolls Stuffed with Mushrooms and Pork • 213

Pork Rib Roast, Tuscan Style • 217

Oven-Roasted Brussels Sprouts with Thyme Butter • 219

California Lime Pie • 220

Navel Oranges with Lavender Syrup • 222

Pears with Blue Cheese, Walnuts, and Honey • 225

Three Citrus Thick-Cut Marmalade • 227

Candied Orange or Lemon Peel • 229

**Farmers' Markets for Health:
Sutter Davis Hospital by Janet Wagner • 233**

Acknowledgments • 234

Index • 236

Foreword

The best part of every week is my trip to the farmers' market. I go straight to the local teahouse to meet my friends before I venture in, and we chat about our market strategy for the day, telling each other what to buy. "Dirty Girl Farms has the best dry-farmed tomatoes this week. Have you tried them yet?" Or "Frog Hollow's Bartlett pears are just reaching their peak!" Or "Have you tasted the new sauerkraut that Culture is making?" There is nothing better than this coming together at the market: It is where I ground myself.

I first fell in love with farmers' markets in France, when I was a college student studying abroad in the 1960s. I was astonished to see the bounty of each season: Farmers came bearing great heaps of produce in every possible color and shape, from tiny *fraises des bois* to tender young asparagus spears to glossy green leaves of chard. In France, I learned, you had to go to the market twice a day—twice *a day!*—to make sure you caught the farmer with the freshest lettuce. These markets seduced me. They were unlike anything I had ever seen in the United States—and they were glimpses of what could be. It was what I wanted in my life, and how I wanted to shop when I first opened Chez Panisse in 1971.

What I came to understand is that the farmers' market is about so much more than just beautiful produce: It creates a direct and vital link between the people who grow our food and the people who eat it, without the middlemen, so money goes straight to the small, local farms that need it most. (Some people call me a farmers' market philanthropist, because I'm so eager to spend!) Just as importantly, the market is the perfect space for people to reconnect with their senses, experiencing aromas, tastes, sounds, the feel of a ripe peach, the beauty of romanesco broccoli. The market is a place where people come to celebrate the rhythm of the seasons and the rich traditions of diversified, sustainable, and local agriculture. This is the simple and universal philosophy that Ann Evans, Annie Main, and the farmers and students in Davis understood from the market's beginnings in 1975, even as the rest of our country was still dominated by big-box supermarkets and industrialized farming. The Davis Farmers Market has long been at the vanguard in this nation, and it has led the way for the thousands of markets that have sprung up around the country over the past forty years. After all these years, I am thrilled that I can now walk out the door of Chez Panisse every Thursday and see a bustling farmers' market right down the block. I feel absolutely certain I would not be able to do this were it not for the pioneering vision of the Davis Farmers Market.

Now more than ever, the Davis Farmers Market is uniquely positioned to effect change—right in the heart of our state, across the river from our capital. I am so excited that the market has partnered with the school district to form a Davis Farm to School Connection—what better way for markets to evolve and lead the country? By bringing food from farms into schools, we are putting edible education at the forefront, bringing children into a new relationship to food—food that is nourishing, and that is grown by a person who cares about the land.

This is the great beauty of the market, the way in which it effortlessly puts us on the right path and we absorb its lessons by osmosis. This is how people have been gathering for centuries—since the beginning of civilization, really. It's something that's instinctive, built into our very nature. In the winter, we find ourselves at the market tasting the cheeses, holding a steaming mug of cider; in summer, we stroll through with a basket of ripe olallieberries. We come to understand that, rain or shine, we can feed ourselves in this elemental and intuitive fashion. This book is a beautiful tribute to the people who have kept this market alive and vibrant for nearly forty years, with every recipe a little love letter to the farmers who grow the ingredients: *soupe au pistou* with fresh shelling beans, fresh pasta with spring peas and asparagus, frisée salad with egg and pancetta. I know that behind these simple recipes, a lot of work and determination has gone into building the market that this book honors. It takes a tremendous amount of effort to make the market grow, to be constantly vigilant about the farmers who come, to provide the best access to shoppers. The Davis Farmers Market is the perfect model of the way in which a market can and should be done—and I am forever grateful for its shining example.

— Alice Waters,
restaurateur, activist, author, and proprietor of Chez Panisse

DAVIS FARMERS MARKET VENDORS

KRISTY LEVINGS OF CACHE CREEK MEAT CO. AT THE MARKET.

JIM ELDON OF FIDDLER'S GREEN FARM IN BROOKS, CALIFORNIA.

CAROL VAIL AND ED MEHL OF V&M FARMS, STRAWBERRY GROWERS IN WATSONVILLE, CALIFORNIA.

MARILYN GARIBALDI OF GARIBALDI FARMS AT THE MARKET.

JOHN BLEDSOE OF BLEDSOE & SON WITH HIS PIGS ON HIS RANCH IN YOLO, CALIFORNIA.

PART I: Introduction

Story of the Davis Farmers Market

The history of the Davis Farmers Market begins with the social awakening of the late 1960s and early 1970s, which set the stage for the establishment of alternative, local food systems. Since then, farmers' markets, led by Davis, a college town in the Sacramento Valley, and by California, have exploded across the country, testimony to that seminal moment in popular history. Today, there are over 7,100 farmers' markets nationwide, and more than 700 of them are in California.

Located in the city's Central Park, the Davis market takes up about one-third of the almost five-acre park on Saturday mornings and a good bit more on Wednesday evenings during Picnic in the Park. It operates under a pavilion built especially for it with public funds, one of the few of its kind in the state, and it draws seven to ten thousand people each week.

These are my memories of how the Davis market, one of the first in California, came together in 1975 and 1976 through the work of a determined band of farmers, college students, and others. It is also the story of how we took the market to the next level through the electoral process, and of how it has become a new platform for educating the community through our local schools.

The story of the market is in part my story. I am a cofounder and have participated in its development over almost four decades, seeing it through its conception, birth, adolescence, and now maturity. Today, the Davis Farmers Market runs two markets in Central Park, as well as the UC Davis Farmers Market and, since June 2011, the Sutter Davis Hospital Farmers Market. I served on the city council that originated the master plan that included a permanent home for the market, and I chaired the Davis Farmers Market Association board of directors, which established the Davis Farmers Market Foundation to fund school and community programs.

Market cofounders Martin Barnes, Jeff and Annie Main, Henry Esbenshade, and I were all students at the University of California at Davis in the late 1960s and early

1970s. We came together through friendship, political activism, the Agrarian Effort, the founding of the Davis Food Cooperative, and a shared mentorship under UC Davis rural sociologist Isao Fujimoto and his Alternatives in Agricultural Research Project.

Isao came to the campus in 1967 from New York's Cornell University, a land-grant college like Davis, to work on the Social Implications of Research project in the Community Development Department. But his more important contribution was his creation of a learning environment relevant to the times. Students flocked to him and his idea of blending community development, environmental sustainability, and political economy. The story of Isao and others like him is fundamental to understanding why this market has a deep parentage and a fierce devotion.

Berkeley's Free Speech Movement took place in 1968, and the first Earth Day followed in 1970. Those heady days spawned societal change across California and the nation. In 1972, Davis held the first election in the state in which students could vote in their campus community, and a new majority was elected to the Davis City Council. Former UC Davis associated student body president Bob Black, Joan Poulos, and Maynard Skinner took office. Black had run on a progressive platform calling for change within the community, including a new bus system, a health system, and a farmers' market. Laurie Hammond and Phil Kitchen, the managers of the first market, worked hard with others to establish the market in Central Park, but it failed in its second year. That failure would provide many lessons for the next attempt to build a market.

Across the Sacramento River from Davis, in Sacramento, the state capital, politics were changing as well. Jerry Brown was elected governor in 1974 and promised sweeping changes. Consumer groups were organized and strong, promoting milk price supports, produce-packing restrictions, and the like. New voices were being heard at the policy table.

In 1976, with a bachelor's degree in consumer food science in hand, I went to work for Brown's activist Department of Consumer Affairs, where I focused on starting food cooperatives in food deserts such as West Oakland, Watts, and San Francisco; on establishing community canneries statewide; and on launching

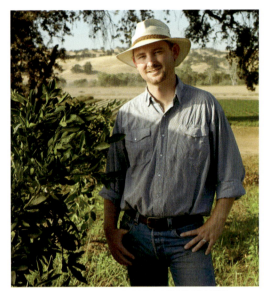

THADDEUS BARSOTTI, CO-OWNER OF CAPAY ORGANIC, AT THE FAMILY FARM IN CAPAY, CALIFORNIA.

JEFF AND ANNIE MAIN OF GOOD HUMUS PRODUCE IN CAPAY, CALIFORNIA.

direct-marketing experiments with state prisons in which the prisons purchased produce directly from farms in the area for their inmate meal programs. I also joined with consumer representatives from around the state to link cooperative movements with direct marketing and farmers' markets.

In that same year, Henry Esbenshade, Martin Barnes, and Annie Main secured approval from the city council to open the Davis Farmers Market in Central Park. Emboldened by the Davis Food Cooperative's promise to buy anything that the farmers couldn't sell, Annie and Jeff Main scoured the county for farmers who were willing to bring their goods to the market. In December, Henry, Martin, and I, along with other co-op enthusiasts, moved the Davis Food Cooperative buying club (three hundred households strong) into its first storefront. Soon after, Martin, Henry, and Annie set up their own farms, eventually becoming Capay Organic, Everything Under the Sun, and Good Humus, respectively, all of which continue to sell at the market today.

The next two years saw even greater strides made. Consumers and new organic farmers began lobbying to change state regulations that restricted farmers' markets and other forms of direct marketing of food. The State Department of Food and Agriculture brought together industry representatives, organic farmers, and consumers to debate the necessary changes, and in time the department adopted regulations that created the nation's first certified farmers' markets. Finally, as long as their products met minimum quality standards and were sold in a market certified by the county agricultural commissioner, farmers could legally sell their products directly to consumers without meeting the usual size, standard pack, and container requirements. George Hellyer and Mark Lleinwand, with the department's Office of Direct Marketing, and Davis resident and longtime Davis Farmers Market board member Les Portello executed the new program.

Over the next decade or so, organic and other small-scale farming grew as demand for what these new farmers could produce swelled. The growth was fueled by people such as Sibella Kraus, first of Chez Panisse and then of Greenleaf Produce, and Georgeanne Brennan and Charlotte Kimball, who founded Le Marché Seeds in 1980. They were responsible for introducing many of the European varieties that are now commonplace, such as red romaine, arugula, Chioggia beets, and Lacinato kale. Pioneer market growers from around the nation contacted them to learn what was newly imported. Among them were growers who were selling at the Davis Farmers Market.

Although the market had grown from just three farmers with boxes of produce on the ground, some eggs, and loaves of bread to a thriving marketplace with a steadily growing number of both vendors and fruit and vegetable cultivars, it was still temporary in the minds of many. Successive market managers, including Annie Main, Solomon Teklu, John Poorbaugh, and Randii MacNear, did the best they could, but it took Randii on her second stint as manager (now going on thirty years) and a vote of the Davis electorate to take the market to the next level: an expanded Central Park and a market pavilion.

Originally constructed in 1937, Central Park (between Fourth and Fifth and B and C streets) is the city's oldest park. The old Lincoln Highway once ran along the park's west side, now B Street, and from 1918 through 1966, the Davis Elementary School stood on the square block next to it. When the school came down, the square block became a gravel parking lot, which it remained until 1986, and ultimately 1990, though not for lack of development efforts. I like to say the land had a will of its own, and I'm sure without that divine intervention, the market would not be what it is today. In this next phase of development, public funding and public policy switched to center stage.

Known as the Arden Mayfair site after a grocery store that was never built, the square block came under city ownership in the 1970s. The purchase, which cost in excess of one million dollars, occurred during Bob Black's tenure on the city council and was made possible with funds secured through federal revenue sharing. In retrospect, Bob Black sees this as a key development in the establishment of the farmers' market, as it kept the space under public control. My council (I served on the council from 1982 to 1990, and as mayor from 1984 to 1986) proposed development of the land in 1984, as a means of strengthening the city's economic base. Former mayor Maynard Skinner led a campaign, Save Open Space (SOS), to block that plan. SOS received a 58 percent majority vote at the ballot box. The council then issued an invitation to design and architecture firms to submit proposals to develop the park extension's master plan. The plan included closing Fourth Street and grassing it over to connect Arden Mayfair to Central Park, making one two-block-long park; constructing a market pavilion to protect vendors and customers from the rain (the first such pavilion in California); and other amenities. Everyone loves the park and pavilion today, but back then there was less consensus, and the final vote was a close three to two.

CoDesign, a local architectural firm founded by landscape architect Mark Francis and architect Jim Zanetto, won the competition to design the park and pavilion and drew up the master plan with input from the community. The plan was implemented over three phases, from 1988 through 1994. CoDesign won national awards for its design of the park and the pavilion.

In 1990, Phase 1 was completed. In 1991, the teen center facility opened (now the U.S. Bicycling Hall of Fame Museum). In 1992, the Davis library building, originally constructed on F Street in 1911, was moved and renovated to become the Hattie Weber Museum of city history. In 1994, Phase 2 of the Central Park expansion opened and it included the now-famous Farmers Market Pavilion, as well as new children's play areas, a water basin art piece, and a water fountain plaza. Co-founder Annie Main was almost in tears when she shared with me her memory of that first Christmas market after the pavilion was completed. It was a cold day and it rained, yet it was a happy day. She confided that she knows politics come and go and cannot be counted on, but that now, at long last, the ambiance the growers had dreamed of had been achieved. The pavilion gave everyone a feeling of permanence. For farmers like Jeff and Annie Main of Good Humus, who rely on farmers' markets for their primary income, it was an enormous personal relief.

Where did the money come from to build out the master plan? It was not included in the SOS initiative, so it fell to my council to find it. Tax increment funding from the recently formed Davis Redevelopment Agency was our answer. In seeking to fulfill a campaign promise to build more affordable, cooperative housing, I had learned from then state assemblyman Tom Hannigan about the tax increment provided through state redevelopment agencies. After heated debate, the council formed the Davis Redevelopment Agency and put the core area, including the park, inside the area eligible for funding.

Today, market shoppers take heart as they watch hundreds of children enjoying the play equipment adjacent to the market. Another favorite of the children is the old-fashioned pedal-powered carousel, which was funded by the community. In 1995, the Davis Educational Foundation (predecessor to today's Davis Farmers Market Foundation) put The Flying Carousel of the Delta Breeze on the north side of the park. Designed by fifth-generation carousel builder William Dentzel, the community painted the beloved flying horses, pigs, and other magical animals. The carousel, overseen by the market, raises funds for school classrooms that sign up to run it for a day, giving them any profits earned during their tenure.

This connection between the Davis schools and the market is stronger now than ever and provides a context for future development. In 2005, I renewed my role with the market by serving on its board of directors. Randii and I agreed that the association needed a tax-exempt public educational foundation, and we knew the one we wanted. The two of us, with the Davis Farm to School Connection steering committee members under the leadership of Dorothy Peterson, had helped the school district add a farmers' market salad bar to its school lunch program in 2001. Conversely, the farm to school group had raised funds for improving recycling at the Davis Farmers Market to mirror a program in the schools. The relationship had worked well, and in 2007, the Davis Educational Foundation became the market's foundation, renamed the Davis Farmers Market Foundation, and Dorothy Peterson became its chair. The market now had a formal way to receive funds for educational programming in the schools and the community.

The market has stayed true to its local roots. Over 70 percent of the vendors come from within a one-hour hour drive of the market, and 50 percent stay year-round. The festivals, such as Pig Day, Fall Festival, and the Village Feast (the latter raises funds for farm-fresh food in the schools), are complemented by Picnic in the Park, which is held weekly spring through fall. This popular evening event offers the public a free space to socialize and picnic, with a basket from home or prepared food from a market vendor, and to listen to live music and shop for produce. The improved educational gardens on the west side (another foundation project) and the market chefs who prepare signature dishes also contribute to the market's success. Sellers with compelling stories, visitors from all over the world, and multigenerational family shoppers create the weekly warp and weft of the market fabric.

But perhaps my friend and market cofounder Annie Main, who has been doing the market for thirty-five years, says it best. She, like her fellow sellers, sees the market from the other side. People held her children when they were babies, and her adult children now sell at the market as a part of Good Humus. She told me that you see many people's lives walk by every Saturday. For example, you notice who gets divorced and who gets married. You also notice who no longer appears and you wonder where they have gone. Have they moved, died, or just lost interest? Part of the job she and other vendors have taken on goes beyond selling: it includes a relationship with their customers.

Longtime market manager Randii MacNear says that the market mirrors the values of the community, which is why it works. At the heart of those values is preserving assets for the generations to come. The last big chunk of the infrastructure went in at the south end of the market in 2000. Like the carousel, it came about through private funding. Known as the Marie Whitcombe Plaza, it was named after Marie Louise (Olsson) Whitcombe, who sold honey at the market in the early days. Local artist Susan Shelton created a ceramic mural with bees and beehives and other market symbols for the dedication and permanent commemoration of the plaza. The late Whitcombe, whose children have sold melons and corn at the market and who donated the funding for these south-side improvements in her honor, is also, like so many market family and friends throughout town, an indelible part of the market's story.

The history of the market, as John Poorbaugh mused, is part fact, part fiction, and part legend. In this history, I have tried to recognize some of those early pioneers who poured their hearts and souls into the founding and building of the market. If I have omitted some, it is not for lack of their contribution. In the end, the market in Davis could be a market in any town where the public good is put to the use of the people, where the surrounding soil is fertile and worked, and where people of different faiths and purposes on the planet are willing to slow down, gather together, and shop while they swap the news.

— Ann M. Evans

RANDII MACNEAR, MARKET MANAGER

REFLECTIONS OF A MARKET MANAGER

It was thirty years ago that I first experienced the magic of being the "one" who arrives to a dark and empty Central Park and brings the Davis Farmers Market to life. At 4:30 a.m. every Saturday morning, week after week, rain or shine, freezing or sizzling hot, it was, and still is, a moment that evokes feelings of gratitude, pride, and pure joy. No one else is present to see me doing this opening ceremony or hear me still wondering each week, "Will they come to market today?"

When you see the Davis Farmers Market nowadays, with its pleasing pistachio-colored pavilion, it is hard to imagine that it all started with a trio of farmers with a few boxes filled with squash and tomatoes, peppers and onions. Those three pioneering organic-farm families were a brave group who all had a similar thought, "Will they come to market if we are here for them?" They did come. Only about thirty customers showed up in the beginning. But they were happy customers, and they gave the farmers hope more would come.

The Davis Farmers Market is proud to have been among the first four certified farmers' markets established in the state. That pride has shaped the market's incredible journey and will continue to do so. Today, thousands of customers come each market day, year after year, because they love what they find and because the market makes them feel hopeful for a world that is real.

When we are at the market, life gets simpler. Children like eating foods that have one word: apple, cherry, carrot. We say hello to neighbors. We offer our kids a juicy, perfectly ripe strawberry. We learn how to make soup. The market nourishes us as human beings, not just because of the farmers' delicious fruits and vegetables but also because the experience rejuvenates our humanity and retools the way we think about the world. We get to take a breath and then we continue on, with renewed hope.

A marketplace is the oldest concept in time for farmers, eaters, and observers. Just as the markets of ancient civilizations were the heart and soul of those communities, so, too, are our modern-day community farmers' markets, especially the Davis market. As of this writing, I have managed the Davis market for some four thousand market days. I am grateful for every one of those moments because I have been the privileged "one"—the one who gets to share the joy of the farmers as they feed their customers, the pride of a community that cherishes its marketplace, and the grateful expressions of customers who appreciate good, healthful food. And now we have *The Davis Farmers Market Cookbook: Tasting California's Small Farms*, a volume of simple, real food that truly celebrates our unique marketplace.

I invite you to our table, to our farms, and, most of all, to share the gratitude and joy of eating from the market. Many people say that family is whoever is sitting around the table with you. Our Davis Farmers Market family now includes you, the reader, and we welcome you.

— Randii MacNear

Seasonality

What is seasonality?

We can sense the seasons and when they change, but what does that mean in terms of the agricultural landscape, of the farms that produce the food we eat?

We know when it is spring because the air is warmer, the days are lengthening, and many of the trees, barren in winter, suddenly show leafy green. Come summer, the days are hot, not just warm. The rolling hills are golden brown and we seek relief from the heat. Fall creeps up on us, but we can feel it in the slight chill of the morning air, the increasingly early twilight, and the drying of the leaves on grapevines and trees. Full-blown winter is cold, the grass is withered and dark brown, the deciduous trees have shed their leaves, and the days are short.

What we eat each season celebrates that time of year. But because the Davis Farmers Market has a particularly rich mix of vendors who farm in diverse growing areas, many crops overlap the seasons. Despite that fluidity, certain characteristics that signify the passing of time on the land remain strong.

Spring is the season of new growth.

In spring, the saps and juices that were dormant in winter begin to flow, and plants put forth tender leaves, shoots, and buds. It is the time of the year we eat tender lettuces, young turnips, radishes, artichokes, asparagus, English peas, and green garlic. We see the first early apricots and cherries. As time passes and the days warm, the lettuces bolt, flower, and set seed. The root crops get fibrous and also go to seed. The artichokes toughen with the heat and longer days and then burst into bright purple flowers. Once-tender asparagus stalks stiffen and emerge as ferns, and the slender bulbs of the green garlic stalks have developed into thick heads, full of individual cloves.

Summer is the season of full growth.

Summer encourages the final cycle of plant growth, producing hearty-fleshed fruiting bodies with seeds. The primary moment of harvest for many of the maturing vegetables, such as squashes, cucumbers, and most eggplants, will be when the seeds are immature. Green beans are also at their tender best when dense and meaty and their seeds are nearly invisible. In contrast, tomatoes, melons, and peppers are ready to be enjoyed when their seeds are fully developed. The mature stone fruits, like peaches, nectarines, plums, and Pluots, flood the market in a multitude of varieties. The pome fruits, apples, pears, and quinces, begin to appear, along with figs and grapes, heralding fall.

Fall is the crossover season.

In the early days of fall, we still have summer's tomatoes, corn, beans, and peppers. But soon, as the days shorten and the temperatures drop, we'll find similarities to the cooler days of spring, with the first crop of fall chicories, lettuces, and leeks. The longer-growing winter squashes, the ones eaten when they have hard skins and fully mature seeds, appear in the market alongside the shelling beans, whose shriveled pods are discarded and fully formed beans are saved and eaten right away or left to dry. Dates, pomegranates, and persimmons make their appearance alongside the pome fruits. Leafy chard, early collards, and spinach all appear in fall but continue deep into winter, as do broccoli, Brussels sprouts, and cauliflower. Cultivated mushrooms are in the market year-round, but fall is the primary time for the wild chanterelles, porcini, and puffballs.

Winter is the dormant season.

Walnuts, almonds, pistachios, pears, apples, and winter squashes have been harvested and are now in the pantry. Hardy root vegetables, like sweet potatoes, are stored away, along with the bulbs—onions, garlic, and shallots. Olives are being harvested and pressed into oil, and we see winter's sturdy greens, like kale and cabbage, filling the market bins. Winter fruits, the citrus that needs chilling days and sun to sweeten, begin to arrive to stay with us until nearly spring. Mandarins, lemons, and oranges come one after the other, different varieties maturing at different times, so there is always something new to savor.

How to Use This Book

Cooking from the market with the seasons in mind is the primary focus of this book, so we have included eight basic recipes that we use over and over again throughout the year, varying them by season. A savory gratin in spring might have peas and artichokes; in summer, eggplant and tomatoes; in fall, mushrooms; and in winter, cauliflower. Fresh pasta is bright in spring with asparagus and in fall with shelling beans. A basic pie recipe follows the seasons, with apricots and cherries in late spring, peaches and nectarines in summer, apples and quinces in fall, and in winter, citrus. Each of the eight basic recipes is accompanied by seasonal suggestions to guide you.

We've also included three basic recipes for homemade stocks: vegetable, chicken, and beef. These are easy to make and will enrich the flavor of your food. Make a batch when you have the time, label it, and store it in the freezer.

We debated whether or not to create seasonal menus for you and decided against it. Instead, we have arranged the chapters by the seasons, and within each chapter we have ordered the recipes by how they fall in a menu: first courses, soups and salads, main dishes, side dishes, and desserts. At the end of each chapter, we have included a few recipes for preserving the season.

Our hope, and our reason for writing this cookbook celebrating the Davis Farmers Market, is to share with you the way we love to cook and to eat, day in and day out, from the market and our gardens in season. We have some basic recipes and some special ones; stock in our freezers; jams, jellies, pickles, and sauces in our pantry; and a good array of spices and other seasonings in our cupboards. We cook with vegetables, fruits, and fish and shellfish in season, along with meats, cheeses, eggs, and grains. It is a simple matrix. The flavors and combinations are endless and endlessly satisfying to us, as we hope they will be to you.

SCOTT STONE OF YOLO LAND AND CATTLE COMPANY ROUNDING UP HIS CATTLE IN DIXON, CALIFORNIA.

LLOYD AND WILLIAM JOHNSON OF LLOYD'S PRODUCE AT THE MARKET.

LUCY AND RAMON CADENA OF CADENA RANCH AT THE MARKET.

FRESH-PRESSED OLIVE OIL—*OLIO NUOVO*—FROM YOLO PRESS.

MIKE MADISON OF YOLO BULB AND YOLO PRESS AT OLIVE MILLING TIME ON HIS FARM IN WINTERS, CALIFORNIA.

PART II: # The Basics

EIGHT RECIPES TO ADAPT TO THE SEASONS

With these eight recipes in hand, you can come to the market and pick out what looks the freshest, the most delicious, and the most tempting, knowing that you have a repertoire of basic dishes in which you can use whatever you buy. These are the recipes, or concepts in some cases, that we use day in and day out throughout the year when we cook from the market.

RISOTTO

Risotto, a classic of the Italian table, is versatile. It can be a main course, a first course, or a side dish, and vegetables, seafood, meats, or herbs can be added to create countless different versions. Five ingredients, stock, rice, cheese, wine, and butter, nearly always come into play, and each is important. (Italian cooks eschew cheese in seafood risottos.) The kind of stock you use can vary but should always be flavorful. The most commonly used rice is short-grain Arborio, though Carnaroli and Vialone Nano, two less frequently encountered varieties, are also good choices. The cheese is classically Parmesan, but other high-quality, full-flavored cheeses, such as Taleggio or pecorino romano, can be used as well. Wine can be white or red depending on the other ingredients, and butter should always be unsalted and of excellent quality. Risotto is easy to make and cooks rather quickly, though you'll have plenty of time to enjoy a glass of wine while you stir.

SEASONAL VARIATIONS
Spring: *Asparagus with tarragon, vegetable or chicken stock, and a dry white wine; or English peas and morel mushrooms and a dry white wine.*
Summer: *Sautéed zucchini or other summer squash with vegetable or beef stock and a dry red wine; or sautéed eggplant and basil and a dry red wine.*

Fall: *Butternut squash with sage and a dry red wine; or sun-dried tomatoes with rosemary and a dry red wine.*
Winter: *Crab or shrimp with vegetable or chicken stock and a dry white wine; or homemade sausage (see page 158) with thyme and a dry red wine.*

Basic Risotto Recipe with Four Kinds of Mushrooms

2 quarts vegetable stock, homemade (page 48) or purchased

8 tablespoons (1 cube) unsalted butter

2 tablespoons extra-virgin olive oil

2 cups chopped mushrooms of four different kinds such as cremini, portabello, shiitake, and oyster

1 yellow onion, finely chopped

2 cups Arborio rice

1 cup dry white wine

⅔ cup shelled English peas (scant 1 pound in the pod)

¾ cup freshly grated Parmesan cheese, plus more for serving

1 tablespoon chopped fresh herb of choice such rosemary, thyme, or sage (optional)

Sea or kosher salt and freshly ground black pepper

1. In a saucepan over medium-high heat, bring the stock to a boil. Reduce the heat to low and maintain at a gentle simmer.

2. In a frying pan over medium-high heat, melt 1 tablespoon of the butter with the olive oil. When the oil and butter are hot, add the mushrooms and sauté until golden brown, about 5 minutes. Remove from the heat and set aside.

3. In a saucepan over medium-high heat, melt 6 tablespoons of the butter. When it foams, add the onion and sauté until almost translucent, 2 to 3 minutes. Add the rice and stir gently until it glistens, about 5 minutes. Reduce the heat to medium, add the wine, and cook, stirring, until it is absorbed. Before the rice starts to stick to the pan, add about 1 cup of the hot stock and stir until it is absorbed. Continue adding the stock about 1 cup at

4   a time, stirring until it is absorbed before adding more. When about half of the stock has been added and absorbed (after about 10 minutes), stir in the mushrooms and peas.

Continue adding the stock about 1 cup at a time and stirring constantly. After about 10 minutes longer, the rice should be done—just tender to the bite but still slightly firm in the center. (You may not need all of the stock.) Stir in the cheese, the remaining 1 tablespoon butter, the herbs (if using), a pinch of salt, and a few grinds of pepper and mix well. Taste and adjust the seasoning with salt and pepper. For a more liquid risotto, add $1/2$ cup stock (or use hot water if you have used up the stock) and stir vigorously for 1 to 3 minutes until creamy. Remove from the heat, cover, and let stand for 5 minutes.

5   Spoon the risotto into a warmed serving bowl or individual shallow bowls or plates. Pass the pepper mill and additional cheese at the table.

Serves 6

PASTA

Pasta dishes vary from culture to culture, but the essence is the same: fresh or dried noodles of various shapes and sizes are cooked until tender and dressed with a sauce or used in a soup, often with the addition of vegetables, herbs, meat, poultry, and/or seafood.

Italian-Style Pasta

Dried pasta, made from durum wheat flour, is fundamental to Italian cooking. In the United States, it has become synonymous with quick-to-fix comfort food, but it can also be quite complex and elaborate. Dried pastas come in many shapes, from long, thin rods, flat, wide ribbons, and short tubes to such fanciful forms as corkscrews, wheels, butterflies, and conch shells. Plus, there are wide, flat, long lasagna noodles for layering and large tubular manicotti (muffs) for stuffing. The sauces that go with all of these choices can be as simple as butter or olive oil with cheese, garlic, and red pepper flakes or as rich as Bolognese meat sauce.

Fresh pasta (see page 69) is easy to make and cooks more quickly than dried pasta. It can be cut into long strips, shaped to make ravioli or cappelletti, or left in sheets for lasagna. Fresh pasta should be paired with a light sauce so as not to overwhelm its delicate texture.

SEASONAL VARIATIONS

Spring: *Peas and asparagus or sautéed artichokes with Parmesan; or fava beans and green garlic with goat cheese.*

Summer: *Grilled sardines with yellow raisins; or fresh tomatoes with basil and burrata cheese; or fresh tomato sauce with garlic and sausage; or sautéed eggplant and summer squash.*

Fall: *Roasted sweet peppers and onions; or basil pesto; or fresh salmon and cream; or broccoli and anchovies.*

Winter: *Dungeness crab and tomato sauce; or pancetta and eggs; or shredded braised beef and its jus with Parmesan; or lemon zest, arugula, and ricotta.*

Basic Pasta Recipe, Italian Style, with Sautéed Onions and Red Sweet Peppers

3 tablespoons extra-virgin olive oil

½ cup minced yellow onion

1 large red sweet pepper, halved, seeded, and thinly sliced lengthwise

Sea or kosher salt and freshly ground black pepper

8 ounces dried fettuccine, spaghetti, or other dried pasta

¼ to ½ cup freshly grated Parmesan cheese

1 Bring a large pot of water to a boil over high heat.

2 While the water is heating, in a frying pan over medium-high heat, warm the olive oil. When it is hot, add the onion and sauté until almost translucent, 2 or 3 minutes. Add the pepper strips and sauté, stirring, until glossy, about 2 minutes. Cover, reduce the heat to low, and cook, stirring occasionally, until the pepper strips are soft and have released their

3   juices, 10 to 15 minutes. Season with a little salt and pepper, then remove from the heat and set aside covered.

3   When the water is boiling, add the pasta and 2 teaspoons salt and stir the pasta to prevent sticking. Adjust the heat to just below a rolling boil and cook, stirring once or twice to prevent sticking, until the pasta is al dente (tender to the bite), 8 to 11 minutes, depending on the size and thickness of the pasta and the package instructions.

4   Drain the pasta and transfer to a warmed serving bowl or platter. Reheat the pepper mixture if necessary and add it to the pasta. Season the pasta with salt and pepper, sprinkle with half of the cheese, and toss well. Serve right away, accompanied with the remaining cheese.

Serves 2 or 3

Asian-Style Pasta

Noodles are one of the most popular foods in Asia. They come in various shapes, sizes, and textures, like the long, brittle bean thread noodles that become slippery and transparent during cooking or the semitransparent rice vermicelli that turn opaque when cooked. Asian noodles are made from rice, wheat, buckwheat, yams, potatoes, mung beans, and more and can be served hot or cold, in stir-fries, soups, or salads. In each case, they lend themselves well to variations throughout the seasons.

In the basic recipe that follows, which calls for tossing noodles with sweet peppers and tofu and a simple sauce, dried Japanese soba noodles, made from a mix of buckwheat and wheat flours, are used, but dried or fresh Chinese wheat noodles or egg noodles can be substituted.

SEASONAL VARIATIONS
Spring: *Stir-fried bok choy, steamed sugar snap peas, and asparagus with a touch of garlic; or stir-fried snow peas or pea shoots and shiitake mushrooms; or tofu and green onions.*
Summer: *Grilled eggplant and fresh chiles; or shredded chicken and carrot; or smoked salmon and steamed yellow squash; or tofu and Thai basil with braised spinach and chopped peanuts.*

Fall: *Stewed loquats and shredded pork with a hint of ginger and lemon zest; or stir-fried Chinese broccoli and walnuts; or red sweet pepper and tofu; or stir-fried eggplant and long beans.*
Winter: *Kumquats and shredded chicken with honey and black sesame seeds; or steamed napa cabbage and shiitake mushrooms.*

Basic Pasta Recipe, Asian Style, with Sweet Peppers and Tofu

12 ounces dried soba noodles

Sauce

3 tablespoons tamari or other Japanese soy sauce

2 tablespoons toasted sesame oil

1 tablespoon mirin (sweet Japanese cooking wine)

1 teaspoon rice vinegar

1 tablespoon peeled and minced fresh ginger

2 teaspoons sugar

1 cup chopped red sweet pepper

1 cup cubed tofu

¼ cup minced fresh cilantro

1 Bring a large pot of water to a boil. Add the noodles, stir to combine, adjust the heat to a steady simmer, and cook until the noodles are tender, about 5 minutes or according to the package instructions. Drain in a colander, rinse under cold running water to halt the cooking, and drain well.

2 To make the sauce, in a bowl, stir together the soy sauce, sesame oil, mirin, vinegar, ginger, and sugar until the sugar dissolves.

3 Transfer the noodles to a serving bowl. Add the red pepper, tofu, cilantro, and sauce to the noodles and toss to mix evenly. Serve at room temperature or chilled.

Serves 4

SAVORY GRATIN

A gratin is essentially a baked dish with a browned topping, usually of seasoned bread crumbs or cheese. A vegetable gratin is one of the most common home-cooked dishes and can be readily varied with the seasons, making it a quick and easy staple. In the basic recipe that follows, the vegetable is cooked and then combined with a cheese sauce; topped with cheese, butter, and bread crumbs; and baked. Including chopped cooked bacon or bits of ham or prosciutto will contribute additional flavor. Alternatively, the cooked vegetables can be drizzled with extra-virgin olive oil, sprinkled with cheese and bread crumbs, and baked. Gratins can also be made with meats or seafood.

SEASONAL VARIATIONS
Spring: *Leeks, green garlic, artichokes, or asparagus and prosciutto.*
Summer: *Eggplant, zucchini (see page 110), Belgian endive, or salmon.*
Fall: *Sweet peppers and onions, beets, or cauliflower.*
Winter: *Broccoli, Brussels sprouts, Swiss chard, or oysters.*

Basic Gratin Recipe with Broccoli

- 1 clove garlic
- 3½ tablespoons unsalted butter
- 3 or 4 broccoli heads, cut into florets (about 3 cups)
- 2 tablespoons all-purpose flour
- 1 cup whole milk
- 1 teaspoon sea or kosher salt
- ½ teaspoon freshly ground black pepper
- ⅛ teaspoon cayenne pepper
- ½ cup shredded Gruyère or Monterey Jack cheese
- ½ cup fresh bread crumbs

1 Preheat the oven to 400°F. Rub a 4- to 5-cup gratin dish or other shallow baking dish with the garlic clove and ½ tablespoon of the butter.

2 Set up a steamer, bring the water to a boil, arrange the broccoli in the steamer rack, cover, and steam until the stems are easily pierced with a fork, about 10 minutes. Remove the broccoli from the steamer and coarsely chop or leave whole if you prefer a chunkier dish. Set aside.

3 In a saucepan over medium-high heat, melt 2 tablespoons of the butter. When it foams, remove from the heat and whisk in the flour to make a paste. Return the pan to the heat and slowly whisk in the milk. Reduce the heat to medium, whisk in the salt, black pepper, and cayenne pepper, and simmer, whisking from time to time, until thickened, 10 to 15 minutes. If necessary, raise the heat slightly to thicken the sauce. Add a little more than half of the cheese, stir until melted, and remove from the heat. Taste and adjust the seasoning with salt and pepper if needed.

4 Transfer the broccoli to the prepared gratin dish and pour the sauce evenly over the top. Stir or lift and turn the broccoli as needed to cover it completely. Sprinkle with the remaining cheese.

5 In a small skillet over medium-high heat, melt ½ tablespoon of the butter, add the bread crumbs, and cook, stirring, until the bread crumbs are golden, 1 to 2 minutes. Sprinkle the bread crumbs evenly over the cheese topping. Cut the remaining ½ tablespoon butter into small pieces and dot the top of the gratin.

6 Bake until a golden brown crust has formed and the sauce is bubbling, about 20 minutes. Serve hot, spooned directly from the dish.

Serves 4

SAVORY TART

Savory tarts are simply savory custards baked in a pastry crust, like a French quiche. They can be plain, with only cheese, eggs, and milk, or they can include one or more other ingredients, such as spinach, bacon, fish, broccoli, or mushrooms. Different cheeses can be used as well, such as Gruyère, Fontina, or Cheddar. Be sure to use whole milk, half-and-half, heavy cream, or a mixture to ensure the custard sets. Also, any vegetables must be cooked and squeezed or pressed dry before they are added so the custard won't be watery.

SEASONAL VARIATIONS

Spring: *Asparagus, peas, artichokes, morel mushrooms, or potatoes.*
Summer: *Swiss chard, spinach, zucchini, eggplant, okra, or salmon.*
Fall: *Mushrooms, leeks, cabbage, or bell peppers.*
Winter: *Onions, collard greens, kale, Swiss chard, or crabmeat.*

Basic Savory Tart Recipe with Chard, Spinach, and Bacon

Crust

2 cups all-purpose flour

½ teaspoon sea or kosher salt

4 tablespoons unsalted butter, frozen and cut into walnut-size pieces

5 to 6 tablespoons ice water

Filling

8 chard leaves, stem ends trimmed

2½ teaspoons sea or kosher salt

1 bunch spinach, tough stems removed

2 slices bacon

2 tablespoons minced yellow onion

3 ounces soft fresh goat cheese

1¼ cups whole milk

1 egg

½ teaspoon freshly ground black pepper

½ tablespoon unsalted butter, cut into small pieces

2 tablespoons freshly grated Parmesan cheese

1 To prepare the crust in a food processor: Combine the flour and salt in a food processor and pulse several times to mix. Scatter the butter over the flour mixture and pulse five to seven times, until the butter is in pea-size balls and covered with flour. Add 5 tablespoons of the ice water and, using ½-second pulses, pulse about five times, until the water is incorporated and the dough comes together in a rough mass. If the dough does not cling together, add the remaining 1 tablespoon ice water and pulse just until combined. Do not overwork the dough or the gluten in the flour will develop and the crust will be tough.

2 To prepare the crust by hand: Combine the flour and salt in a bowl and stir to mix. Scatter the butter over the flour mixture and, using two knives, your fingers, or a pastry blender, work the butter into the flour mixture until the butter is in pea-size balls covered with flour. Add the ice water, 1 tablespoon at a time, and stir and toss with a fork until the dough comes together in a rough mass. You may not need all of the ice water. Do not overwork the dough or the gluten in the flour will develop and the crust will be tough.

3 Gently shape the dough into a firm ball, lightly dust the ball with flour, and then flatten the ball into a thick disk. Cover the disk with plastic wrap and place in the refrigerator for 30 minutes or in the freezer for 10 minutes. Meanwhile, preheat the oven to 400°F.

4 On a lightly floured work surface, roll out the dough into a 10- or 11-inch round (to fit a 9- or 10-inch tart pan) $1/4$ to $1/3$ inch thick, moving and flouring the disk two or three times to avoid sticking, handling the dough as little as possible, and working quickly so the dough remains cool. Place the rolling pin on the far edge of the round and roll the round up onto the pin. Position the pin over a 9- or 10-inch tart pan with a removable bottom and unroll the dough round, centering it over the pan. Press it into the bottom and sides of the pan, letting the dough overlap the rim. Trim the overlap to within a generous $1/4$ inch of the rim and crimp the edges. Line the pastry with a sheet of aluminum foil, pressing it against the sides and bottom of the pan, and fill with pie weights or dried beans.

5 Bake until the edges are firm but not golden, about 10 minutes. Remove the weights and foil, prick the bottom in several places with the tines of a fork, and continue to bake until the bottom is opaque, 2 to 3 minutes longer. Transfer to a wire rack and let cool completely. Reduce the oven temperature to 375°F.

6 To make the filling, place a large pot filled with water over high heat and bring to a boil. Reduce the heat to medium-high, add the chard leaves and 2 teaspoons of the salt, and cook until the chard stalks are soft, about 10 minutes. Add the spinach and cook until thoroughly wilted but still bright green, about 5 minutes longer. Drain in a colander and place under running cold water until cool enough to handle. With your hands, squeeze the chard and spinach dry, then chop finely. Set aside.

7 In a frying pan over medium heat, fry the bacon until crisp, about 8 minutes. Transfer to paper towels to drain. Pour off all but 1 tablespoon of the fat from the pan and return the frying pan to medium-high heat. Add the onion and the chopped chard and spinach and cook, stirring often, until no liquid is visible, about 3 minutes. Add the goat cheese and

8. In a bowl, whisk together the milk, egg, the remaining $1/2$ teaspoon salt, and the pepper until blended. Crumble the bacon and add it along with the spinach mixture, mixing well. Pour the mixture into the prebaked tart shell. Dot the top with the butter and sprinkle with the Parmesan cheese.

9. Bake until the top is deeply golden and slightly puffed, 30 to 35 minutes. Let cool in the pan on a wire rack for at least 10 to 15 minutes before serving. To unmold the tart, place the tart pan on a large can or similar object and let the rim fall away. Using a wide spatula, slide the tart off of the pan bottom and onto a flat serving plate, or leave the tart on the pan bottom and place it on the plate. Serve warm or at room temperature, cut into wedges.

Serves 6 to 8

ROASTED VEGETABLES

Roots, tubers, and squashes, coated with extra-virgin olive oil laced with chopped fresh herbs such as rosemary, thyme, and sage, are wonderful roasted in a hot oven. Whole or chopped garlic cloves deepen the flavor of whatever you are roasting, and the longer you roast the garlic, the more likely it is to caramelize, making it sweet and soft. Choose a deep, medium-size baking dish of glass, ceramic, or earthenware or a baking pan of enameled cast iron or other heavy material. Most vegetables are ready in about an hour.

SEASONAL VARIATIONS
Spring: *Beets, young carrots, fennel, young turnips, or new potatoes.*
Summer: *Eggplants, summer squashes, or sweet potatoes.*
Fall: *Winter squashes, beets, carrots, or celery root.*
Winter: *Turnips, rutabagas, parsnips, or yams.*

Basic Roasted Vegetables Recipe with Spring Vegetables

1 bunch beets	15 cloves garlic, peeled but left whole
1 bunch turnips	1/3 to 1/2 cup extra-virgin olive oil
1 bunch carrots	1 to 2 teaspoons sea salt
2 to 3 pounds new potatoes	Leaves from 1 fresh rosemary sprig, about 5 inches long, finely chopped (about 2 teaspoons)
2 yellow onions, quartered through the stem end	

1 Preheat the oven to 400°F.

2 Trim off the green tops of the beets, turnips, and carrots. Discard the carrot tops and reserve the beet and turnip tops for another use. Chop the beets, turnips, carrots, and potatoes into bite-size pieces and put into a large bowl. Add the onions and garlic and mix well. Add the olive oil and toss to coat the vegetables evenly. Season with the salt and rosemary and toss again. Transfer the vegetables to a heavy baking dish or pan large enough to accommodate them in a snug single layer.

3 Roast the vegetables for 15 minutes. With a spatula, scrape the bottom of the baking dish to ensure nothing is burning or sticking. Reduce the oven temperature to 350°F and continue to roast until the vegetables are tender when pierced with a fork, 45 minutes to 1 hour. Every 20 minutes or so, check the baking dish to make sure the vegetables are not sticking, scraping the bottom again with the spatula. Serve hot or at room temperature.

Serves 6 to 8

VEGETABLE FRICASSEE

A classic fricassee is made with pieces of chicken that are cooked but not browned in oil or butter and then finished by simmering in a white sauce, with or without vegetables. A vegetable fricassee, however, can be as simple as cooking one or more vegetables, chopped, sliced, or slivered, in oil or butter and seasoning with herbs, salt, and pepper. They can be served on their own as a main dish, or as a base for fish, meat, or poultry.

SEASONAL VARIATIONS
Spring: *Morel mushrooms, peas, and asparagus (optional heavy cream); or fava beans, green garlic, and artichoke hearts.*
Summer: *Zucchini and corn; or corn and okra; or green beans, corn, and oyster mushrooms.*
Fall: *Fresh shelling beans and green beans; or butternut squash and sweet peppers.*
Winter: *Brussels sprouts, walnuts, and cabbage; or red cabbage and chestnuts; or kale, chard, and collards with cream and red pepper flakes.*

Basic Vegetable Fricassee Recipe with Corn and Sweet Pepper

2 to 3 tablespoons extra-virgin olive oil	1 red sweet pepper, seeded and chopped
1 clove garlic, chopped	1 teaspoon chopped fresh oregano
2 tablespoons chopped yellow onion	½ teaspoon sea or kosher salt
2 cups corn kernels	¼ teaspoon freshly ground black pepper

1 In a frying pan over medium heat, warm the olive oil. When it is hot, add the garlic and onion and cook, stirring, until the onion is translucent, 2 to 3 minutes. Add the corn and red pepper and cook, stirring, until the pepper is tender, about 2 minutes. Stir in the oregano, salt, and pepper and mix well. Serve hot.

Serves 2 or 3

RUSTIC SWEET TART

A rustic sweet tart is fruit wrapped in a free-form pastry. Nothing could be simpler. Not even a tart pan is required. The pastry should be flaky and melt in your mouth, and because the tart is shallow, the crust is as important as the seasonal fruit that it showcases. A bit of honey or a few sprinkles of sugar will bring out the natural sweetness in the fruit. Select fruit that is ripe but not too ripe or it will collapse in the heat of the oven.

SEASONAL VARIATIONS

Spring: *Pitted cherries, halved apricots, or berries of all kinds.*
Summer: *Sliced stone fruits such as peaches, nectarines, or plums, alone or in combination with berries.*
Fall: *Sliced quinces or apples or halved figs.*
Winter: *Sliced apples or kiwifruits.*

Basic Rustic Sweet Tart Recipe with Apples

Crust

- 1½ cups all-purpose flour
- 1 tablespoon sugar
- ¼ teaspoon sea or kosher salt
- ½ cup (1 cube) plus 2 tablespoons unsalted butter, frozen and cut into walnut-size pieces
- 4 tablespoons ice water
- ¼ teaspoon vanilla or almond extract (optional)

Filling

- 3 cups thinly sliced apples
- 3 to 4 tablespoons honey, warmed until fluid if necessary
- 2 tablespoons unsalted butter, cut into small pieces
- 1 egg, lightly beaten, for egg wash

1 To prepare the crust in a food processor: Combine the flour, sugar, and salt in a food processor and pulse several times to mix. Scatter the butter over the flour mixture and pulse five to seven times, until the butter is in pea-size balls and covered with flour. Add the ice water and the vanilla (if using) and, using $1/2$-second pulses, pulse just until the water is incorporated and the dough comes together in a rough mass. Do not overwork the dough or the gluten in the flour will develop and the crust will be tough.

2 To prepare the crust by hand: Combine the flour, sugar, and salt in a bowl and stir to mix. Scatter the butter over the flour mixture and, using two knives, your fingers, or a pastry blender, work the butter into the flour mixture until the butter is in pea-size balls covered with flour. Add the ice water, 1 tablespoon at a time, and stir and toss with a fork until the dough comes together in a rough mass. If using, add the vanilla with the last addition of ice water. Do not overwork the dough or the crust will be tough.

3 Gently shape the dough into a firm ball, lightly dust the ball with flour, and then flatten the ball into a thick disk. Cover the disk with plastic wrap and place in the refrigerator for 30 minutes or in the freezer for 10 minutes. Meanwhile, preheat the oven to 400°F. Line a baking sheet with parchment paper.

4 On a lightly floured work surface, roll out the dough into a 12-inch round $1/8$ to $1/4$ inch thick, moving and flouring the disk two or three times to avoid sticking, handling the dough as little as possible, and working quickly so that the dough remains cool. Place the rolling pin on the edge of the round and roll the round up onto the pin. Position the pin over the prepared baking sheet and unroll the dough round, centering it on the pan.

5 Arrange the apple slices in concentric circles on the dough round, leaving a 2-inch border uncovered. Drizzle the honey evenly over the apple slices. Dot the apples with the butter.

6 Fold the 2-inch pastry border up over the apples, making loose pleats as you work your way around the edge and leaving the center open. Using a pastry brush, lightly coat the pleated edge with the egg, which will give the baked crust a shiny, golden brown finish.

7 Bake until the crust is golden brown, about 40 minutes. The apples should still be slightly firm. Let cool for at least 15 minutes on the pan on a wire rack. Using a wide spatula, slide the tart onto a serving plate. Serve warm or at room temperature, cut into wedges.

Serves 8

FRUIT PIE

This basic recipe will work for almost any type of fruit except citrus. The dough, which can be made by hand or in a food processor, comes out flaky, tender, and rich—perfect for pairing with any fruit as well. If you want to sweeten the pastry a bit, sprinkle in a little sugar. Flour or quick-cooking (minute) tapioca can be used interchangeably as the thickening agent for the filling, or they can be used together.

SEASONAL VARIATIONS
Spring: *Apricots (see page 83) or strawberries and rhubarb.*
Summer: *Peaches, nectarines, plums, or berries such as blueberry, olallieberry, loganberry, or blackberry (for all berries except blueberries, double the amount of thickening agent and use 5 to 6 cups fruit).*
Fall: *Apples or quinces (omit the thickening agent for both).*
Winter: *Apples or pears (omit the thickening agent for both).*

Basic Fruit Pie Recipe with Cherries

Crust

1½ cups all-purpose flour

½ teaspoon sea or kosher salt

½ cup (1 cube) unsalted butter, frozen and cut into walnut-size pieces

5 tablespoons ice water

Filling

4 cups (about 2 pounds) sweet or sour cherries, pitted

⅔ to 1 cup sugar, depending on ripeness of fruit

3 tablespoons quick-cooking tapioca or all-purpose flour

1½ tablespoons fresh lemon juice

½ teaspoon almond extract (optional)

1 tablespoon unsalted butter, cut into small pieces

1 egg, lightly beaten, for egg wash

1 To prepare the crust in a food processor: Combine the flour and salt in a food processor and pulse several times to mix. Scatter the butter over the flour mixture and pulse five to seven times, until the butter is in pea-size balls and covered with flour. Add the ice water and, using $1/2$-second pulses, pulse just until the water is incorporated and the dough comes together in a rough mass. Do not overwork the dough or the gluten in the flour will develop and the crust will be tough.

2 To prepare the crust by hand: Combine the flour and salt in bowl and stir to mix. Scatter the butter over the flour mixture and, using two knives, your fingers, or a pastry blender, work the butter into the flour mixture until the butter is in pea-size balls covered with flour. Add the ice water, 1 tablespoon at a time, and stir and toss with a fork until the dough comes together in a rough mass. Do not overwork the dough or the gluten in the flour will develop and the crust will be tough.

3 Gently gather together the dough and then divide it into two portions, one twice as large as the other (the larger portion, or two-thirds of the dough, will be the bottom crust, and the smaller portion, or one-third of the dough, the top crust). Gently shape each portion into a firm ball, dust each ball lightly with flour, and then flatten each ball into a thick disk. Cover each disk with plastic wrap and place in the refrigerator for 30 minutes or in the freezer for 10 minutes. Meanwhile, preheat the oven to 450°F and prepare the filling.

4 To make the filling, place the cherries in a large mixing bowl and sprinkle with the sugar, tapioca, lemon juice, and almond extract (if using). Stir gently until blended. Set aside.

5 On a lightly floured work surface, roll out the large dough disk into an 11-inch round (to fit a 9-inch pie pan) $1/4$ to $1/3$ inch thick, moving and flouring the disk two or three times to avoid sticking, handling the dough as little as possible, and working quickly so the dough remains cool. Place the rolling pin on the far edge of the round and roll the round up onto the pin. Position the pin over a 9-inch pie pan and unroll the dough round, centering it over the pan. Press it into the bottom and sides of the pan. Do not trim the overhanging edges. Roll out the small dough disk into a 10-inch round $1/4$ inch thick and leave whole if making a double-crust pie or cut into $3/4$- to 1-inch-wide strips if making a lattice-topped pie.

6 Pour the filling into the pastry-lined pie pan. Dot the filling with the butter. If making a double-crust pie, fold the top crust into quarters. To make air vents, cut out a small triangle, about $1/2$ inch long, on each of the two folded sides. Carefully unfold the crust over

7. the filling, making sure it is centered. The triangles will now be diamond shapes. Using a sharp knife, trim the edge of the top and bottom crusts, leaving a 1/2-inch overhang. Fold the overhang under and pinch or flute to create an attractive edge. Using a pastry brush, brush the top crust with the egg wash.

7. If making a lattice-topped pie, using a sharp knife, trim the edge of the bottom crust, leaving a 1/2-inch overhang, and then fold the overhang under. Lay half of the strips 3/4 to 1 inch apart over the filling. Fold back every other strip halfway. Lay a strip across the unfolded strips, positioning it perpendicular to them and in the center of the pie, then unfold the folded strips over it. Now, fold back the strips that were left lying flat, place a second dough strip 3/4 to 1 inch away from the first perpendicular strip, and again unfold the folded strips. Repeat with the remaining strips to complete the lattice. Using the sharp knife, trim off any overhanging pastry, press the ends of the strips firmly to the bottom crust, and pinch or flute the edge. Using a pastry brush, brush the lattice with the egg wash.

8. Bake the pie for 10 minutes. Reduce the oven temperature to 350°F and continue to bake until the crust is golden brown, about 40 minutes longer. Let cool on a wire rack for at least 15 minutes. Serve warm or at room temperature, cut into wedges.

Serves 8

THREE BASIC STOCKS TO MAKE FROM SCRATCH

Homemade stocks are not a necessity, but they do have a better flavor than store-bought. They are also a good way to use vegetable trimmings that you might otherwise discard, such as leek greens and mushroom stems. We both like to make big batches of stock and then freeze them in practical-size containers of 4 to 6 cups each. Of course, not everyone will have homemade stock on hand all the time. Fortunately, a number of good-quality stocks and broths are available commercially. If possible, select a product that is fat free, organic, and low in sodium.

Vegetable Stock

2 quarts water

4 carrots, cut into 3-inch pieces

3 celery stalks, cut into 3-inch pieces

2 leeks, white and green parts, cut into 3-inch pieces

2 yellow onions, quartered through the stem end

8 ounces fresh mushrooms, or 2 tablespoons dried mushrooms

2 bay leaves

½ bunch fresh flat-leaf parsley

4 or 5 fresh thyme sprigs

Sea or kosher salt and freshly ground black pepper

1. In a large stockpot over medium high-heat, bring the water to a boil. Add the carrots, celery, leeks, onions, mushrooms, and herbs and return to a boil. Reduce the heat to low, cover, and simmer for about 45 minutes. Uncover and simmer for 25 minutes longer. Season with salt and pepper.

2. Remove from the heat and strain through a chinois or a colander lined with cheesecloth. Let cool, then cover and refrigerate for up to 4 days or freeze for up to 6 months.

Makes 6 to 7 cups

Chicken Stock

4 quarts water

1 whole chicken, about 3 pounds, or 3 pounds bony chicken parts such as backs and wings

1 large yellow onion, coarsely chopped

4 carrots, coarsely chopped

3 celery stalks with leaves, coarsely chopped

5 fresh flat-leaf parsley sprigs, 3 fresh sage sprigs, 2 fresh rosemary sprigs, or 5 fresh thyme sprigs, or a combination, tied together with cotton string

1 In a large stockpot over medium-high heat, bring the water to a boil. If using a whole chicken, remove the giblets and neck from the cavity. Reserve the giblets for another use. If you have bought a chicken with its feet on, leave them on. Add the whole chicken and its neck (or the chicken parts), onion, carrots, celery, and herbs to the boiling water and bring back just to a gentle simmer, skimming off any foam that rises to the surface with a slotted spoon. Adjust the heat to low to maintain a gentle simmer, cover, and simmer for 30 minutes.

2 If using a whole chicken, remove the chicken from the pot, re-cover the pot, and continue to simmer. Let the chicken cool for 15 minutes, then remove the meat from the bones in large pieces where possible (breast, thigh, leg) and reserve the meat for another use. Return the carcass to the pot and continue to simmer, uncovered, for at least 2 hours or up to 4 hours.

3 Remove from the heat. Using a slotted spoon or a skimmer, remove and discard the large solids, then strain the stock through a chinois or a colander. If using a colander, line the colander with cheesecloth and strain the stock again. Let cool, then cover and refrigerate until chilled. Remove from the refrigerator and, using a large spoon, lift off and discard the congealed fat on the surface. Use immediately, or cover and refrigerate for up to 4 days or freeze for up to 6 months.

Makes 3 to 3½ quarts

Beef Stock

6 pounds meaty beef shanks, cracked (ask the butcher to do this)

6 cloves garlic, peeled but left whole

8 fresh flat-leaf parsley sprigs

5 fresh thyme sprigs

2 dried bay leaves, or 4 fresh bay leaves

15 black peppercorns

2 yellow onions, coarsely chopped

1 leek, white and green parts, coarsely chopped

2 carrots, coarsely chopped

2 celery stalks, coarsely chopped, or 1 small head celery root, peeled and coarsely chopped

1 cup hot water

1. Preheat the oven to 450°F.

2. Place the shanks in a roasting pan in which they fit without crowding and roast, turning occasionally, until nicely browned on all sides, about 1½ hours.

3. Transfer the shanks to a large stockpot and set aside the roasting pan with the pan juices. Add cold water to cover the shanks generously and bring to a boil over medium-high heat. Add the garlic, parsley, thyme, bay leaves, and peppercorns and reduce the heat to low. Simmer gently, uncovered, skimming off any froth that rises to the surface and adding water as needed to maintain the original level, for 2 hours.

4. Meanwhile, place the roasting pan with its pan juices over medium-high heat and add the onions, leek, carrots, and celery. Cook the vegetables, stirring them often and being careful they do not scorch, until they caramelize, 15 to 20 minutes. Remove from the heat.

5. When the shanks have simmered for 2 hours, add the caramelized vegetables to the pot. Return the roasting pan to medium-high heat, add the hot water, bring to a simmer, and deglaze the pan, stirring to dislodge any browned bits from the pan bottom. Add the contents of the roasting pan to the stockpot and continue to simmer, uncovered, until the flavors have developed and blended, about 1 hour longer.

6. Remove from the heat. Using a slotted spoon or a skimmer, remove and discard the large solids, then strain the stock through a chinois or a colander. If using a colander, line the colander with cheesecloth and strain the stock again. Let cool, then cover and refrigerate until chilled. Remove from the refrigerator and, using a large spoon, lift off and discard the congealed fat on the surface. Use immediately, or cover and refrigerate for up to 5 days or freeze for up to 6 months.

Makes 3 to 4 quarts

LYDIA CASTILLO OF BUSALACCHI FARMS AT THE MARKET.

SONG VUE OF VUE FAMILY FARM AT THE MARKET.

JAYMES LUU OF FAT FACE AT THE MARKET.

MIKE MCDONALD OF MCDONALD ORCHARDS AND HIS HONEY BEES IN BROOKS, CALIFORNIA.

DIANNE MADISON OF YOLO BULB AND YOLO PRESS AT THE MARKET.

PART III: The Recipes

ANNIE MAIN OF GOOD HUMUS PRODUCE AT THE MARKET.

Spring
the Season of New Growth

In spring, the days lengthen and the temperature rises, the necessary conditions for germination and growth. The warming soil bursts with new life, and the traditional spring vegetables start to appear at the market: new leafy greens, the first stalks and buds, tender roots and tubers, and pods plump with delicate, immature seeds. Soon the year's first stone fruits and soft berries will show up, along with morel mushrooms. With more daylight hours, chickens begin laying again, spring lamb becomes available, and, with luck, the anchovy and sardine swarms reappear in the Pacific, where they will be caught and brought to the market.

The market stalls are bursting with produce, and a shopping excursion is likely to tempt buyers with butterhead, Batavia, romaine, and loose-leaf lettuces; thin-stemmed, dark green spinach; delicate notch-leaved arugula; and bunches of chives and tarragon. Bundles of fat asparagus spears, slim leeks, and green garlic; stacks of prickly tipped artichokes; and baskets of sweet strawberries line vendors' tables. So, too, do bunches of radishes and carrots and pyramids of new potatoes, all of them captured from beneath the soil. Fava beans, English peas, and sugar snap peas are abundant, and by late May the first cherries appear.

Because the season's vegetables and fruits are so tender, spring dishes are often the easiest and least time-consuming to prepare. Most need little or no cooking, resulting in dishes such as roasted or steamed asparagus, a risotto of peas and morel mushrooms, or fresh spring rolls. Winter, with its hearty greens, sturdy root crops, and long braises, seems a long way off.

Warm Leek Salad with Oil-Cured Olives and Eggs

One evening our friend, French-born plein air painter Philippe Gandiol, served us this dish, one of his mother's recipes. It is well suited for a first course in early spring, when leeks are in the market, though asparagus can be used as well. The wine vinegar and mustard dressing is so intensely flavored that no salt or pepper is needed.

2 bunches leeks (about 6 large leeks or 12 baby leeks)

½ cup extra-virgin olive oil

3 tablespoons Dijon mustard

2 tablespoons red wine vinegar

1 hard-boiled egg, peeled and finely chopped

½ cup oil-cured black olives, pitted and chopped (about ¼ cup)

1. Trim the ends of the leek greens, leaving 4 to 5 inches of green intact, and trim off the roots. If using large leeks, cut each leek in half lengthwise and rinse thoroughly. If using baby leeks, leave whole and rinse thoroughly.

2. Pour water to a depth of 2 inches into a steamer pan, put the steamer rack in place, lay the trimmed leeks on the rack, and cover the steamer. Place over medium heat, bring to a boil, and steam until the leeks are tender to a fork, about 5 minutes for large leeks and 2 minutes for baby leeks. If you don't have a steamer, pour about 1 cup water into the bottom of a sauté pan, place over medium heat, and bring to a boil. Add the leeks, cover, turn down the heat to a simmer, and cook until the leeks are tender to a fork, about 5 minutes for large leeks and 2 minutes for baby leeks.

3. While the leeks are cooking, make the dressing. In a small bowl, stir together the olive oil, mustard, and vinegar.

4 When the leeks are ready, remove them from the steamer (or sauté pan) and hold under cold running water for a few seconds to halt the cooking and to secure the bright green color. Drain the leeks well and transfer them to an oval platter, arranging them so that they are all facing the same direction. With a sharp knife, cut down crosswise through the leeks every 1 to 1½ inches.

5 Pour the dressing over the leeks while they are still warm. Sprinkle the chopped egg on top of the leeks in stripes. Arrange stripes of chopped olive on either side of the egg stripes. Serve warm or at room temperature.

Serves 4 to 6

Deviled Eggs with Tarragon

We both favor purist versions of deviled eggs. In other words, we like the rich, savory flavor of the fresh egg to dominate. Our recipes are quite similar, though Georgeanne adds a bit of Dijon mustard to the yolks. To maximize the flavor of the freshly ground pepper, I warm a handful of peppercorns in a dry, covered pan over low heat to release their volatile oils, and then I grind them the old-fashioned way, with a mortar and a pestle, though a pepper mill works well, too.

6 eggs

¼ cup mayonnaise

Sea or kosher salt and freshly ground black pepper

3 tablespoons minced fresh tarragon or chives

1. Put the eggs in a saucepan, add cold water to cover, and place over high heat. As soon as the water is boiling, remove the pan from the heat, cover it, and let the eggs stand for 20 minutes.

2. Remove the eggs from the pan and rinse under cold running water until cool. Peel the eggs and cut them in half lengthwise. Gently lift out the yolks, dropping them into a bowl. Set the whites, hollow side up, on a large plate or tray. Using a fork, mash the yolks with the mayonnaise until thoroughly combined and smooth. Season with salt and pepper. Add the tarragon and fold in gently.

3. Using a teaspoon, fill each egg cavity with some of the yolk mixture, mounding it slightly. Serve right away or cover and refrigerate for up to 4 hours before serving.

Makes 12 stuffed eggs

Flatbreads with Spring Onions and Feta

I've used this simple dough recipe for years, and Ann agrees it is easy and versatile. The dough can be rolled or pulled into rectangles, rounds, or whatever shape you like. The toppings vary throughout the seasons, and the garnished flatbreads can be served as an appetizer, a bread accompaniment, or even a main dish. The spring onions, with their plump bulbs and tender greens, can be found at numerous market vendors. They add their own delicate flavor and bright color.

Dough

- 1 envelope (about 2½ teaspoons) active dry yeast
- 1 cup warm water (105°F)
- ½ teaspoon sugar
- 1 teaspoon sea or kosher salt
- 3 tablespoons extra-virgin olive oil
- 2½ to 3 cups all-purpose flour
- 2 tablespoons rice flour

Topping

- 3 bunches spring onions
- 2 tablespoons extra-virgin olive oil
- 4 to 6 ounces feta cheese, crumbled
- 2 tablespoons minced fresh thyme
- ½ to 1 teaspoon sea or kosher salt
- ½ teaspoon freshly ground white or black pepper
- 2 to 3 tablespoons chopped pancetta, homemade (page 192) or purchased (optional)

1 To make the dough, in a small bowl, sprinkle the yeast over the warm water, add the sugar, and let stand until foamy, about 5 minutes.

2 In a food processor, combine the yeast mixture, salt, 2 tablespoons of the olive oil, and about 2½ cups of the flour. Pulse just until the mixture comes together in a soft ball of dough, adding more flour, a little at a time, if the mixture seems too wet. The dough should be neither too sticky nor too dry.

3 Gather the dough into a ball, transfer to a floured work surface, and knead until smooth and elastic, about 7 minutes. Shape into a smooth ball.

4 Oil a large bowl with the remaining 1 tablespoon oil, add the dough ball to the bowl, and turn the ball to coat it evenly with the oil. Cover the bowl with a damp cloth, place it in a warm, draft-free area, and let the dough rise until doubled in size, $1\frac{1}{2}$ to 2 hours.

5 If you are using a pizza stone, place it on the lower rack of the oven and preheat the oven to 500°F. If you have a convection setting on your oven, use it.

6 Lightly dust 1 or 2 large rimless baking sheets with the rice flour, which helps the flatbreads to slide easily. Punch down the dough and turn it out onto a lightly floured work surface. Divide the dough into two or four equal portions. Using a floured rolling pin, roll out each portion into a round or rectangle no more than $\frac{1}{4}$ inch thick. Transfer to the rice flour–covered baking sheet(s).

7 To make the topping, trim off the roots from the spring onions, then chop all of the white bulb and half of the greens of each onion. Brush the dough rounds or rectangles with about 1 tablespoon of the olive oil. Sprinkle the cheese, onions, thyme, salt, pepper, and pancetta (if using) evenly over the tops and then drizzle with the remaining tablespoon olive oil.

8 If using a pizza stone, slide 1 large or 2 small flatbreads onto it. If not, place the baking sheet directly on the lower rack of the oven. Bake until the edge of the crust is golden brown and the onions are beginning to turn golden. The edge of the crust should be crisp and firm when tested with a fingertip or fork. This will anywhere take from 10 to 15 minutes. Using a wide spatula, transfer the flatbread(s) to a cutting board. Repeat with the remaining flatbread(s). Cut into wedges or rectangles and serve.

Makes two 12- to 14-inch round or 8-by-14-inch rectangular flatbreads, or 4 smaller flatbreads; serves 4

Fava Bean Soup with Pancetta

Ann and I plant favas in our gardens every year, often sharing seeds and always sharing any interesting recipe discoveries. This recipe is based on one I read in an old French cookbook, and the taste is the very essence of favas: rich, meaty, and a little earthy. The pancetta garnish is a nice touch, though the soup could just as well be served unadorned. The fava beans need to be shelled and then peeled, which is time-consuming but worth both the effort and the minutes. April and May are when the fava beans are most abundant in the market.

1-inch-thick slice pancetta, homemade (page 192) or purchased, finely chopped

2½ pounds fava beans in the pod

3 cups chicken stock, homemade (page 48) or purchased

¼ teaspoon sea or kosher salt

¼ teaspoon white pepper

1 tablespoon crème fraîche

1. In a small frying pan over medium-high heat, fry the pancetta just until crisp, about 2 minutes. Using a slotted spoon, transfer to paper towels to drain.

2. Shell the fava beans. You should have 2 to 2½ cups beans. Bring a saucepan filled with water to a boil over high heat. Drop the shelled favas into the boiling water and leave for 30 seconds, then drain. When the beans are cool enough to handle, slip off the tough outer skin of each bean, slitting the skin with the tip of a sharp knife or your thumbnail.

3. In a saucepan over medium-high heat, bring the stock to a simmer. Add the beans, reduce the heat to low, cover, and simmer until they are tender to the bite. The younger the beans the more quickly they will cook. It may take 5 minutes or up to 20 minutes. Remove from the heat and let cool slightly.

4. Working in batches if necessary, transfer the beans and stock to a food processor or blender and purée until smooth. Strain through a fine-mesh sieve into a clean saucepan. Place over medium heat and bring to just below a simmer. Add the salt and pepper, then taste and adjust the seasoning if needed. Stir in the crème fraîche.

5. Ladle the soup into warmed bowls and garnish with the crisp pancetta. Serve hot.

Serves 4

Italian Stuffed Artichokes

When the market is full of artichokes, fresh from the cool Central Coast where they thrive, I like to buy big ones to stuff, similar to the ones I tried in Italy many years ago during a buying trip for Le Marché Seeds, my onetime company. The freshly torn bread absorbs the vinegar, olive oil, and seasonings to make a light, flavorful stuffing, and the coarser the bread, the better. This dish makes an exceptional first course, one that takes a bit of convivial time to eat.

4 medium to large artichokes

1 cup water

4 cups fresh bread crumbs, made from a coarse country bread such as ciabatta or a rustic baguette

5 tablespoons red wine vinegar

½ cup minced fresh flat-leaf parsley (about 1 bunch)

2 cloves garlic, minced (optional)

½ teaspoon sea or kosher salt

½ teaspoon freshly ground black pepper

1 teaspoon fresh lemon juice

2 to 3 tablespoons extra-virgin olive oil

1. Cut off the stem flush with the base and the top one-third (the prickly leaf ends) of each artichoke. Pour water to a depth of about 3 inches into a steamer pan, put the rack in place, and bring the water to a boil over high heat. Place the artichokes, stem end up, on the rack, reduce the heat to medium, cover, and steam until the base of an artichoke offers little resistance when pierced with the tines of a fork, about 30 minutes. The timing will depend on the size and maturity of the artichokes.

2. Remove the artichokes from the steamer and set aside until cool enough to handle. Then, using a spoon, scoop out the central leaves from each artichoke, removing the thistles and any furry bits, to make a cavity about 1½ inches wide. Set the artichokes aside.

3. In a bowl, combine the water and bread crumbs and stir to moisten the crumbs evenly. Let stand just long enough to soften the bread, anywhere from 15 seconds to several minutes, depending on how dry the bread is and how coarse the crumbs are. Squeeze the bread crumbs dry and transfer to a clean bowl.

4. Add the vinegar, parsley, garlic (if using), salt, pepper, lemon juice, and 2 tablespoons of the olive oil to the bread and mix well. Taste and adjust the seasoning with salt and pepper if needed. The mixture will appear fluffy but should be dense enough to hold its shape when squeezed into a ball. Add up to 1 tablespoon additional oil if needed to achieve the correct consistency.

5. Spoon about ¼ cup of the stuffing into the cavity of an artichoke. Pry back a layer of the leaves and tuck ½ teaspoon or so of the stuffing at the base of each leaf in the layer. Pry back another layer and repeat. Continue until you have filled all of the layers. The artichoke will expand like a flower. Repeat with the remaining 3 artichokes.

6. Cover the artichokes with plastic wrap and refrigerate for at least 2 hours or up to 8 hours before serving. Let stand at room temperature for 30 minutes to 1 hour before serving.

Serves 4

Fresh Spring Rolls with Thai Dipping Sauce

This is a fresh, easy, no-cook dish that I taught Georgeanne to make. The rolls can be vegetarian, as they are here, or the tofu can be replaced with shrimp, or both tofu and shrimp can be used. The spring roll wrappers, sometimes labeled rice paper or rice paper rounds, are thin, opaque, brittle disks made from either rice flour or a mixture of rice flour and tapioca flour. You can buy them at Asian grocery stores and in many supermarkets in the international foods section.

Dipping Sauce

½ cup water

¼ cup sugar

½ cup red wine vinegar or rice vinegar

1 tablespoon soy sauce

2 teaspoons red pepper flakes

Spring Rolls

12 round spring roll wrappers, 8½ inches in diameter

1 head red leaf lettuce, separated into leaves

1½ pounds bean sprouts

1 carrot, peeled and cut into matchsticks

1 (14-ounce) package firm tofu, cut into ½-inch cubes

Leaves from 12 fresh mint sprigs

1 bunch green garlic or green onions, including tender green tops, finely chopped

6 to 8 dried Chinese black mushrooms, soaked in warm water to cover for about 30 minutes to soften, drained, stems discarded, and sliced (optional)

Fresh cilantro sprigs for garnish

1 To make the sauce, in a saucepan over medium heat, combine the water and sugar and bring to a boil, stirring until the sugar dissolves, about 1 minute. Remove from the heat, add the vinegar, soy sauce, and red pepper flakes, and stir well. Let cool before serving.

2 To make the spring rolls, set out the wrappers and all of the other ingredients on a work surface where you can reach them easily. You will be filling 12 rolls, so you may want to portion the ingredients into 12 uniform piles so that all of the rolls will get an equal amount of filling. Lay a damp kitchen towel on the work surface. Fill a wide, shallow bowl with hot water. Place 1 spring roll wrapper in the water until softened and quite limp, 15 to 25 seconds, then transfer it to the towel, laying it flat.

3 Place a lettuce leaf flat on the wrapper. Arrange some bean sprouts about 2 inches in from the side nearest to you, creating a row about 2 inches wide and $4\frac{1}{2}$ inches long. Stack some carrot, tofu, mint, green garlic, and mushroom slices (if using) on top of the bean sprouts, being careful not to add too much. The stack should be no more than 2 inches high. Turning up the edge nearest you, begin rolling the wrapper tightly around the filling, then fold in the sides and continue rolling snugly until you reach the opposite edge. Moisten the edge of the wrapper with water to create a strong seal. Place on a platter, seam side down. Repeat with the remaining wrappers and filling ingredients. Cover with a damp towel and set aside in a cool place until serving, no more than 1 hour.

4 To serve, garnish the platter with the cilantro and set out on the table. Divide the sauce among small individual bowls and provide each diner with a bowl.

Makes 12 rolls; serves 6

Fresh Rag Pasta with Peas and Asparagus

This main-dish fresh pasta is made in a food processor, then rolled out into sheets by hand, with the pasta attachment on a stand mixer, or with a hand-cranked pasta machine. Ann uses a stand mixer, and I use a pasta machine, probably because one summer night in Nice, while eating outside at an Italian restaurant, I could see one of the kitchen staff turning out long lengths of near-translucent pasta sheets, order by order, using a hand-cranked machine bolted onto a wooden table. The pasta sheets, rolled by any one of the three methods, can be cut into pappardelle, fettuccine, or lasagna, or they can be torn into pieces, as they are here. The delicate springtime sauce of tender peas and asparagus is a perfect match for the featherlight pasta.

Pasta Dough

1½ to 2 cups all-purpose flour

1 teaspoon extra-virgin olive oil

2 eggs

Vegetables

1 pound asparagus

2 pounds English peas, shelled

To Finish

2½ teaspoons coarse sea or kosher salt

2 tablespoons extra-virgin olive oil or melted unsalted butter

¼ teaspoon freshly ground black pepper

2 tablespoons minced fresh flat-leaf parsley

¼ cup freshly grated Parmesan cheese

1 To make the pasta dough, in a food processor, combine 1½ cups of the flour, the olive oil, and the eggs and process until soft crumbs form that can be pressed together into a ball. If it is too wet, add more flour, a little at a time. If it is too dry, add a little water. The dough should not be sticky.

2 Turn the dough out onto a lightly floured work surface and knead vigorously until smooth and satiny, about 7 minutes. Shape into a ball, cover with an overturned bowl, and let rest for 30 minutes.

3. Lightly flour a couple of large kitchen towels or baking sheets for holding the pasta sheets. Set up your pasta machine according to the manufacturer's instructions. Set the rollers at the widest setting. Divide the ball of dough into balls the size of large walnuts. Slip all but 1 ball back under the bowl. Flatten the ball into a disk and turn the crank to pass it through the rollers. Repeat twice. Move the rollers to the next narrowest setting and again pass the dough through the rollers. Continue to pass the dough through the rollers, narrowing them each time, until you pass it through the next to narrowest setting. Transfer the pasta sheet—it should be thin enough to see your hand through it—to a floured towel or baking sheet and repeat with the remaining pasta balls.

4. Alternatively, on a lightly floured work surface, roll out the pasta dough as thinly as possible and transfer to a floured towel or baking sheet. Again, when it is lifted, you should be able to see your hand through it.

5. If you are not cooking the pasta right away, sprinkle the pasta sheets with flour and cover loosely with a towel. They will keep for up to 1 hour. Just before you are ready to cook the pasta, tear the sheets into $1\frac{1}{2}$- to 2-inch pieces to make the "rags."

6. To prepare the vegetables, bend each asparagus spear near its base until it snaps. Discard the fibrous bases and trim the snapped ends on the diagonal. Slice the tender spears on the diagonal into $\frac{1}{2}$-inch pieces.

7. Fill a large pot three-fourths full with water and bring to a boil over high heat. Add the asparagus and cook until tender to a fork but still bright green, about 2 minutes. Using a slotted spoon or wire skimmer, remove the asparagus and rinse them under cold running water to halt the cooking. Drain well, pat dry, and set aside. Add the peas to the boiling water and cook for 30 seconds. Using the slotted spoon or skimmer, remove the peas from the water and rinse under cold running water to halt the cooking. Drain well, pat dry, and set aside.

8. To finish, if the water is not still at a rolling boil, return it to a boil over high heat. Add $1\frac{1}{2}$ teaspoons of the salt and half of the pasta pieces, stir well, reduce the heat to medium-high, and cook until tender, about 2 minutes. Using the slotted spoon or skimmer, lift the pasta from the water, allowing it to drain well, and place on a platter. Repeat with the remaining pasta. (If your pot is not large, you will need to cook the pasta in three or more batches.) Drizzle the pasta with 1 tablespoon of the olive oil and toss to coat evenly. Keep warm.

9 In a frying pan over medium heat, heat the remaining 1 tablespoon olive oil. When it is hot, add the asparagus, peas, the remaining 1 teaspoon salt, and the pepper and stir for about 30 seconds, just to warm the vegetables through.

10 Divide the pasta among warmed individual plates. Top each portion with one-fourth of the vegetables and sprinkle with the parsley and Parmesan cheese, dividing them evenly and tucking a few vegetables among the ragged pasta pieces. Serve at once.

Serves 4

Young Lamb with Spring Vegetables

Although today it is available year-round, in the past, spring was the traditional time for lamb. In France and Italy, young lamb is still paired with the first flush of early spring vegetables in a braise or stew to celebrate the season. For this version, Ann and I chose succulent lamb shoulder chops, and we finish the vegetables by braising them in butter. At the market in spring, young turnips are especially sweet, whether they are the white or the pink- or purple-topped varieties.

4 lamb shoulder chops	1 bunch small turnips, golf ball size
3 tablespoons extra-virgin olive oil	5 cups water
1 teaspoon kosher or sea salt	2 teaspoons coarse sea salt
½ teaspoon freshly ground black pepper	1½ pounds small fingerling potatoes
4 fresh sage sprigs, crushed	2 tablespoons unsalted butter
Vegetables	½ teaspoon freshly ground black pepper
1 bunch small carrots, 4 to 5 inches long	8 ounces English peas, shelled

1 Place the lamb chops in a shallow baking dish and drizzle with the olive oil, turning the chops several times to coat well. Rub the chops with the salt, pepper, and sage. Set aside to marinate for at least 30 minutes or up to 2 hours.

2 Prepare a medium-hot fire in a wood or charcoal grill, preheat a gas grill to medium-high, or preheat the broiler.

3 Trim off all but ½ inch of the greens from the carrots, then peel the carrots. Trim off all but ½ inch of the greens from the turnips but do not peel. In a large saucepan, bring the water to a boil over high heat. Add 1 teaspoon of the salt.

4 Add the carrots, turnips, and potatoes to the boiling water, reduce the heat to medium, and cook until the vegetables offer only slight resistance to the tines of a fork, 7 to 10 minutes for the carrots and turnips and 12 to 15 minutes for the potatoes. As the vegetables are ready, remove them from the pan with a slotted spoon and set aside. (The vegetables can be cooked up to 1 hour in advance before continuing.)

5 To finish the vegetables, in a sauté pan or frying pan large enough to hold all of the vegetables in a single layer, melt 1½ tablespoons of the butter over medium-high heat. When it foams, add the carrots, turnips, and potatoes, reduce the heat to medium-low, and sprinkle the vegetables with the remaining 1 teaspoon salt and the pepper. Gently cook the vegetables, turning them as needed, until glistening and slightly golden, about 10 minutes. Add the peas and the remaining ½ tablespoon butter during the last 5 minutes of cooking. Cover and remove from the heat.

6 Place the lamb chops directly over the fire and cook, turning once, for about 3 minutes per side for rare or about 5 minutes per side for medium. Or place on a broiler pan, slide under the broiler about 4 inches from the heat source, and broil, turning once, using the same timing. Transfer to a warmed platter and accompany with the vegetables.

Serves 4

Chicken Braised in White Wine with Peas

In spring, along with many market shoppers, we buy big bags of English peas from vendors whose farms are in the cool climates where peas thrive. Peas cooked with lettuce is a classic French preparation in which the lettuce provides just enough moisture for the peas to cook and adds a little something extra, yet takes nothing away from the pure sweet taste of the fresh peas. At the market, Cache Creek Meat Co. sells a variety of different chicken breeds, whole or in parts.

6 chicken thighs

6 chicken drumsticks

1 teaspoon coarse sea or kosher salt

½ teaspoon freshly ground black pepper

2 tablespoons extra-virgin olive oil

1 yellow onion, finely chopped

3 cloves garlic, finely chopped

1 cup dry white wine such as Sauvignon Blanc or Pinot Grigio

1 cup chicken stock, homemade (page 48) or purchased

1 bay leaf

1 tablespoon minced fresh oregano, or 1 teaspoon dried oregano

1 to 2 tablespoons Dijon mustard

Peas

2 bunches green onions

1 tablespoon extra-virgin olive oil

1 large head romaine lettuce, leaves separated and chopped

1 to 2 tablespoons chicken stock, homemade (page 48) or purchased

3 pounds English peas in the pod, shelled

½ teaspoon coarse sea or kosher salt

¼ teaspoon freshly ground pepper

1 To prepare the chicken, season the chicken pieces on all sides with the salt and pepper, rubbing them in well. In a deep, wide frying pan or Dutch oven large enough to hold all of the pieces in a single layer, warm the olive oil over medium-high heat. When it is hot, add the chicken and brown, turning as needed, until golden on all sides, about 10 minutes. (Or, if necessary, brown the pieces in two batches to avoid crowding.)

2 Transfer the chicken to a plate. Pour off all but about 1 tablespoon of the fat from the pan and return the pan to medium-high heat. Add the onion and garlic and sauté until the onion is translucent, 2 to 3 minutes. Pour in the wine and deglaze the pan, stirring to scrape up any browned bits from the pan bottom. Cook until the liquid is reduced to about ½ cup, then add the stock, bay leaf, and oregano and bring to a boil. Return the chicken to the pan, cover, reduce the heat to low, and simmer gently until the chicken is easily pierced with the tines of a fork and opaque throughout, about 30 minutes.

3 Using a slotted spoon or tongs, transfer the chicken to a plate and keep warm. Remove and discard the bay leaf. Stir 1 tablespoon of the mustard into the pan juices over medium heat. Taste and add more mustard or more wine if desired. Simmer for a few minutes, then return the chicken to the pan along with any juices that have collected on the plate and spoon the pan sauce over the chicken to coat evenly. Remove from the heat and cover to keep warm.

4 To cook the peas, trim the roots from the green onions, then finely chop the white of each onion and half of the greens. In a wok or a large, deep frying pan over medium-high heat, warm the olive oil. When it is hot, add the lettuce and green onions and toss to mix. Add the stock, reduce the heat to low, cover, and cook until the lettuce is wilted, about 5 minutes. Add the peas, stir well, cover, and cook until the peas are tender, 3 to 5 minutes if young and slightly longer if more mature. Season with the salt and pepper, then taste and adjust the seasoning if needed. Transfer the peas to a warmed serving bowl.

5 Transfer the chicken to a warmed platter, spoon the mustardy pan sauce over the top, and serve at once. Accompany with the peas.

Serves 4 to 6

CRYSTAL MCCULLAGH OF MISSION FRESH FISH AT THE MARKET.

Baked Whole Cod with Ginger, Carrots, and Green Onions

It can be a bit intimidating to cook a large, whole fish, not because it is difficult but because we do it infrequently. We have an increasingly wide variety of large, whole fish available at the market nowadays, so mastering the technique is worth it. When selecting a fish, look for bright eyes and skin so slippery that the fish is difficult to hold—two strong indicators of freshness. Plan on 8 to 12 ounces of fish per person. In this dish, the firm white flesh becomes delicately perfumed with ginger and onion. Sometimes we like to bake the same type of fish with tomatoes, onions, and olives, giving it the scent and flavors of the Mediterranean.

1 whole cod, 3 to 3½ pounds	1 bunch green onions
2 teaspoons canola oil	3 carrots, peeled
1 teaspoon coarse sea or kosher salt	2-inch piece fresh ginger
½ teaspoon freshly ground black pepper	

1. Preheat the oven to 350°F.

2. If the fish has not already been cleaned, gut it by making a slit along the belly, from the gills to the tail, with a sharp knife. Remove the entrails and discard. Rinse the cavity thoroughly and pat dry. Rub the fish all over, inside and out, with the canola oil. Then rub the fish all over, inside and out, with the salt and pepper. Place the fish in a large baking dish.

3. Trim off the roots of the onions and carrots and cut them on the diagonal into long strips. Peel the ginger and cut into matchsticks. Put about half of the onions and half of the ginger inside the fish cavity and strew the remainder over the top of the fish along with the carrots. Cover the baking dish with foil.

4. Bake the fish until the flesh flakes easily when tested with a knife, 35 to 40 minutes. To test, insert the knife between the backbone and the top fillet; the flesh should pull away from the bone easily, and flakes should be visible. Using a wide metal spatula or two smaller spatulas, transfer the fish to a platter.

5   To fillet the fish, with a sharp knife, make a cut along the dorsal fin, from the head to the tail. Then make one cut to separate the fillet from the head, and a second cut to separate the fillet from the tail. Using two spoons or a spatula, lift off the top fillet, either first cutting it in half lengthwise or leaving it whole, and set it aside on a plate or platter. Now, lift off the central bone in a single piece to reveal the bottom fillet. Cut the fillets as necessary and divide evenly among individual plates.

6   Serve the fish hot, accompanied with a little of the onion, carrots, and ginger, if desired.

Serves 4

Baby Fingerlings with Thyme Blossoms

Zuckerman Family Farms in San Joaquin County is at the market year-round, and its stand always has potatoes, including heirloom varieties. In spring, however, many of the vendors have freshly dug small potatoes as well. Georgeanne and I both grow a variety of herbs and use the blossoms in our cooking, usually thyme or sage flowers in spring and rosemary or winter savory blooms in winter. Although the herb blossoms are headlined here, I really think it is the olive oil that makes this dish. I always use one of the several California extra-virgin olive oils sold at the market for this recipe.

3 pounds fingerling potatoes

¼ cup extra-virgin olive oil

¼ cup fresh thyme or other herb blossoms

2 teaspoons sea or kosher salt

1. Preheat the oven to 400°F. Line a rimmed baking sheet with parchment paper.

2. In a large bowl, combine the potatoes and olive oil and stir to coat the potatoes evenly. Add the thyme blossoms and salt and stir and toss to mix. Pour the potatoes onto the prepared baking sheet, arranging them in a single layer.

3. Roast the potatoes until tender to a fork, 25 to 30 minutes. Transfer to a platter and serve hot.

Serves 8

Green Garlic Flan

Only a short window is open each spring during which green garlic—that is, immature garlic—is available at the market. The cloves and heads have not yet formed, which means the garlic is mellow and mild and its texture is crisp. Together we devised this delicate savory custard with a silky texture and the merest hint of garlic. The individual custards make a special side dish for a beef or pork roast, or you can combine them with a salad for an unusual first course.

4 green garlic stalks

2 cups heavy cream

½ teaspoon coarse sea or kosher salt

¼ teaspoon freshly ground black pepper

½ teaspoon minced fresh thyme

2 whole eggs plus 1 egg yolk

1. Cut off the garlic stalks and discard. Peel off the tough outer skin of the garlic heads and quarter the heads.

2. In a saucepan over medium-high heat, bring the cream to a simmer. Be careful not to let it boil. When the cream is steaming hot, add the green garlic, salt, pepper, and thyme and immediately remove the pan from the heat. Let stand for 30 minutes to allow the flavors to infuse the cream. Taste the cream. If a stronger garlic flavor is desired, let stand for another 30 minutes.

3. Preheat the oven to 325°F. Fill a teakettle with water and bring to a boil.

4. In a small bowl or spouted measuring cup, lightly whisk the whole eggs and egg yolk just until blended. Pour about ¼ cup of the egg mixture into the warm cream mixture while whisking constantly. Add the remaining egg mixture, whisking constantly until well mixed.

5. Using a chinois or a fine-mesh sieve lined with cheesecloth, strain the custard into a spouted measuring cup or pitcher. Divide the custard evenly among eight 3-ounce ramekins.

6 Remove the teakettle from the heat. Place the ramekins in a large baking dish and pour the boiling water into the dish to reach halfway up the sides of the ramekins. Carefully transfer the baking dish to the oven and bake until a knife inserted into the middle of a flan comes out clean, about 30 minutes. The flans will be lightly browned on top. Remove the baking dish from the oven and then remove the ramekins from the water bath. Let cool to room temperature.

7 The flans can be served at this point, or the ramekins can be covered with plastic wrap and refrigerated for up to 24 hours. If refrigerated, bring to room temperature before serving.

8 To serve, run a thin-bladed knife along the inside of a ramekin to loosen the custard. Invert a plate over the ramekin and, holding the plate and ramekin firmly together, invert them so the flan drops onto the plate. Lift off the ramekin (it will be browned side down). Repeat with the remaining ramekins and serve.

Serves 8

Old-Fashioned Apricot Pie

Among the many farmers who bring apricots of many varieties to the market are Jeff and Annie Main of Good Humus Produce, located in the wonderfully named Hungry Hollow valley. They are longtime friends of both mine and Georgeanne's, and they helped start the Davis Farmers Market. According to family lore, one of the first things Jeff and his father did at Good Humus was to plant a Blenheim apricot orchard.

Crust

1½ cups all-purpose flour

½ teaspoon sea or kosher salt

½ cup (1 cube) unsalted butter, frozen and cut into walnut-size pieces

5 tablespoons ice water

Filling

4 pounds apricots, halved and pitted (about 4 cups)

⅔ cup sugar

¼ cup all-purpose flour

3 tablespoons quick-cooking tapioca

1½ tablespoons fresh lemon juice

1 tablespoon unsalted butter, cut into small pieces

1 egg, lightly beaten, for egg wash

1 To prepare the crust in a food processor: Combine the flour and salt in a food processor and pulse several times to mix. Scatter the butter over the flour mixture and pulse five to seven times, until the butter is in pea-size balls and covered with flour. Add the ice water and, using ½-second pulses, pulse just until the water is incorporated and the dough comes together in a rough mass. Do not overwork the dough or the gluten in the flour will develop and the crust will be tough.

2 To prepare the crust by hand: Combine the flour and salt in bowl and stir to mix. Scatter the butter over the flour mixture and, using two knives, your fingers, or a pastry blender, work the butter into the flour mixture until the butter is in pea-size balls covered with flour. Add the ice water, 1 tablespoon at a time, and stir and toss with a fork until the dough comes together in a rough mass. Do not overwork the dough or the gluten in the flour will develop and the crust will be tough.

3 Gently gather together the dough and then divide it into two portions, one twice as large as the other (the larger portion, or two-thirds of the dough, will be the bottom crust, and the smaller portion, or one-third of the dough, the top crust). Gently shape each portion into a firm ball, dust each ball lightly with flour, and then flatten each ball into a thick disk. Cover each disk with plastic wrap and place in the refrigerator for 30 minutes or in the freezer for 10 minutes. Meanwhile, preheat the oven to 450°F and prepare the filling.

4 To make the filling, place the apricots in a large bowl and sprinkle with the sugar, flour, tapioca, and lemon juice. Stir gently until well blended. Set aside.

5 On a lightly floured work surface, roll out the large dough disk into a 11-inch round (to fit a 9-inch pie pan) $1/4$ to $1/3$ inch thick, moving and flouring the disk two or three times to avoid sticking, handling the dough as little as possible, and working quickly so the dough remains cool. Place the rolling pin on the far edge of the round and roll the round up onto the pin. Position the pin over a 9-inch pie pan and unroll the dough round, centering it over the pan. Press it into the bottom and sides of the pan. Do not trim the overhanging edges. Roll out the small dough disk into a 10-inch round $1/4$ inch thick and leave whole if making a double-crust pie or cut into $3/4$- to 1-inch-wide strips if making a lattice-topped pie.

6 Pour the filling into the pastry-lined pie pan. Dot the filling with the butter. If making a double-crust pie, fold the top crust into quarters. To make air vents, cut out a small triangle, about $1/2$ inch long, on each of the two folded sides. Carefully unfold the crust over the filling, making sure it is centered. The triangles will now be diamond shapes. Using a sharp knife, trim the edge of the top and bottom crusts, leaving a $1/2$-inch overhang. Fold the overhang under and pinch or flute to create an attractive edge. Using a pastry brush, brush the top crust with the egg wash.

7 If making a lattice-topped pie, using a sharp knife, trim the edge of the bottom crust, leaving a $1/2$-inch overhang, and then fold the overhang under. Lay half of the strips $3/4$ to 1 inch apart over the filling. Fold back every other strip halfway. Lay a strip across the unfolded strips, positioning it perpendicular to them and in the center of the pie, then unfold the folded strips over it. Now, fold back the strips that were left lying flat, place a second dough strip $3/4$ to 1 inch away from the first perpendicular strip, and again unfold the folded strips. Repeat with the remaining strips to complete the lattice. Using the sharp knife, trim off any overhanging pastry, press the ends of the strips firmly to the bottom crust, and pinch or flute. Using a pastry brush, brush the lattice with the egg wash.

8 Bake the pie for 10 minutes. Reduce the oven temperature to 350°F and continue to bake until the crust is golden brown, about 40 minutes longer. Let cool on a wire rack for 30 minutes to 1 hour before serving. Serve warm or at room temperature.

Serves 8 to 10

Black Cherries in Pinot Noir Gelatin

In late May and in June, the market is flooded with locally grown cherries, and after eating them out of hand to satiate my immediate appetite, I turn to a simple dessert. I'm intrigued by the many ways gelatin can be used, and so I took this opportunity to create this simple yet sophisticated dessert, which Ann and I think captures the season. It can be served with a drizzle of crème fraîche or a dollop of whipped cream.

1 envelope (about 2½ teaspoons) powdered gelatin

2 cups Pinot Noir

¾ cup sugar

4 cups pitted black cherries

2 teaspoons fresh lemon juice

1 Line a 4-by-6-inch loaf pan or similar mold with plastic wrap, smoothing any wrinkles and allowing the plastic wrap to overhang the edges by a few inches. The plastic wrap helps when it comes time to unmold the gelatin. Or, have ready eight to ten small ramekins or other molds.

2 In a small bowl, sprinkle the gelatin over ¼ cup of the wine and allow to soften for about 3 minutes. In a small saucepan over medium heat, combine 1 cup of the wine and the sugar and bring to a simmer, stirring until the sugar dissolves. Reduce the heat to low, add the gelatin mixture, and stir just until the gelatin is dissolved. Do not allow the gelatin to boil. Add the remaining ¾ cup wine, stir well, remove from the heat, and let cool to room temperature.

3 Put the cherries in the prepared pan and pour the wine mixture over them. Cover with the overhanging plastic wrap and refrigerate overnight. Or, divide the cherries evenly among the ramekins and pour the wine mixture over them, dividing it evenly. Cover each ramekin with plastic wrap and refrigerate overnight.

4 To unmold the large mold, using the plastic wrap, lift it out of the loaf pan and place on a cutting board. Using a sharp knife, cut the mold crosswise into 8 uniform slices and place on individual plates. To unmold the individual molds, invert a small plate over a ramekin and, holding the plate and ramekin firmly together, invert them so the gelatin drops onto the plate. Lift off the ramekin. Repeat with the remaining ramekins. If the gelatin does not release from the ramekins, set the ramekins in a shallow pan of hot water for no more than a few seconds and then invert again as directed. Serve chilled.

Serves 8

Apricot Jam

On the tail end of cherry season, apricots arrive in the market, and it is time to make jam. Georgeanne and I started making jam before we left college. Back then I used to can three to four hundred quarts a year of sauces, pickles, jams, and chutneys. Now I make about one hundred quarts a year, but not all at one time like I once did.

You will need five pint canning jars with lids and rings, a large canning kettle with a rack and cover (or a large, wide pot with a wire rack and cover) for the water bath, a large, heavy nonreactive pot for cooking the jam, canning tongs, and a ladle.

5 pounds apricots, halved and pitted

½ cup water

4 cups sugar, or as needed

¼ cup fresh lemon juice

1 To set up the water bath, fill the canning kettle with water (the water must be deep enough to cover the jars by 1 to 2 inches) and bring to a boil over high heat. If you don't have a canning kettle, use a large, wide pot and put a wire rack in the bottom of the pot before you fill it with water. Once the water boils, you can turn off the heat and then return it to a boil just before you put the jars in the kettle.

2 Meanwhile, wash the canning jars in hot, soapy water and rinse well. Place the jars in a large saucepan, add water to cover generously, and bring to a boil over medium-high heat. Boil for 15 minutes, then turn off the heat and leave the jars in the hot water until you are ready to fill them. Fill another saucepan half full with water and bring to a boil over medium-high heat. Add the canning lids and rings and boil for 5 minutes. Turn off the heat and leave the lids and rings in the hot water until needed. Put two or three small saucers in the freezer.

3 Taste an apricot to see if the batch is sweet or tart. In the nonreactive pot over medium heat, combine the apricots and water and heat just until the mixture begins to boil, about 15 minutes. Skim off any foam that forms on top. Stir in 4 cups sugar if the apricots are sweet or slightly more if they are tart, then add in the lemon juice. Bring the mixture to a rolling boil and cook, stirring continuously, until thickened, 12 to 15 minutes.

4 Remove from the heat and quickly skim off any additional foam. Test the jam for jelling by placing a teaspoon of it on a chilled saucer. If it develops a skin after 1 minute, it is ready to jell. If not, return the jam to the heat, boil for 5 minutes longer, and retest.

5 Just before the jam is ready, using tongs, transfer the jars to a work surface. Return the water in the canning kettle to a boil. Ladle the hot jam into the hot, sterilized jars, filling them to within 1/2 inch of the rim. You may not need all of the jars. With a clean, damp cloth, wipe the rim of each jar. Place a lid on the rim and then screw on a ring, being careful not to screw it on too tightly. Using canning tongs, put the filled jars into the rack of the canner and lower the rack into the boiling water. If you are using a large, wide pot, use the canning tongs to lower the jars onto the rack in the bottom of the pot, making sure the jars do not touch. Return the water to a rolling boil, reduce the heat slightly, cover, and boil for 5 minutes.

6 Cover a work surface with a folded towel. Using the canning tongs, transfer the jars to the towel, spacing them a few inches apart. As the jars begin to cool, you may hear popping sounds, which is the sound of the lids sealing. The lids should be indented. When the jars are completely cool, after at least 12 hours, check the seal on each jar by pressing on the center of the lid. If it remains indented, the seal is good. If it does not, refrigerate the jar and use the jam within 1 month.

7 Label the jars with the contents and date and store in a cool, dry place for up to 1 year.

Makes 4 to 5 pints

Pickled Onions

Once you start pickling your own onions, you'll discover how each variety has its own distinct taste. In spring, the onions you'll see at the market are freshly harvested, with moisture still in the skins. By the time the onions are cured, the skins will be papery. All of them can be pickled. Use these on salads, with stewed beans or roasted meats, or as a condiment for hot dogs or hamburgers. Use the beet if pickling yellow onions that you would like to turn red.

5¼ cups water

6 to 7 medium-size yellow or red onions, thinly sliced (about 12 ounces sliced)

1¼ cups white wine vinegar

2 tablespoons sugar

¼ red beet (optional)

Few black peppercorns

1½ teaspoons coarse sea salt

3 bay leaves

3 small dried red chiles

1. Wash 3 pint jars in hot, soapy water and rinse well. Place the jars in a large saucepan, add water to cover generously, and bring to a boil over medium-high heat. Boil for 15 minutes, then turn off the heat and leave the jars in the hot water until you are ready to fill them. Just before the onions are ready, using tongs, transfer the jars to a work surface.

2. In a saucepan over high heat, bring 2 cups of the water to a boil. Add the onions, reduce the heat to medium, blanch for 2 minutes, and drain into a colander.

3. In another saucepan over medium heat, combine the remaining 3¼ cups water, the vinegar, sugar, beet (if using), peppercorns, and the salt and bring to a boil. Reduce the heat to low, cover, and simmer for 5 minutes. Remove from the heat and discard the beet, if used. Add the onions, submerging them. Let stand for 1 minute.

4. Using a slotted spoon, transfer the onions to the hot pint jars, dividing them evenly and packing them snugly. Add 1 bay leaf and 1 chile to each jar, and ladle the hot brine into each jar, filling to within ½ inch of the rim. Cover with lids and let cool to room temperature.

5. Once the jars are cool, refrigerate them. The onions will keep for up to 4 months. For the best flavor, let them sit for 1 week before serving to give the brine time to do its work.

Makes 3 pints

VIN MAISON

Making vin maison, *or farmhouse wine, which is wine that has been fortified with alcohol and sugar and then flavored with fruits, spices, or herbs, is an old French tradition that remains popular today. The wines vary with the seasons, which is part of their charm. In spring,* vin maison *is made with cherries for* vin de cerise; *in summer with peaches for* vin de pêche; *and in winter with oranges for* vin d'orange. *The recipes vary from home to home but the basic method remains the same. The infused, fortified wines are easy to make and fun to serve, typically over ice as an aperitif.*

VIN DE CERISE

1 pound sweet or sour ripe cherries

1 (750-ml) bottle dry red wine

1½ cups sugar

¼ cup kirsch, cherry-infused Cognac, or vodka

Discard any blemished cherries. Stem the cherries and then pit each cherry by gently squeezing it until the pit pops out, leaving the cherry whole. In a large stainless-steel or other nonreactive saucepan over medium-high heat, combine the cherries, wine, and sugar and bring the mixture to a gentle boil, stirring to dissolve the sugar. Cook for about 5 minutes.

Remove from the heat and transfer the mixture to a clean, dry heatproof jar or crock with a wide mouth. Add the kirsch, cover with a lid or several layers of cheesecloth, and let stand in a cool, dark place for 2 days.

Using a slotted spoon, scoop out the cherries and reserve to serve over vanilla ice cream or pound cake for dessert. Line a funnel with a few layers of cheesecloth and place in a clean, dry bottle. Pour the wine through the funnel into the bottle. Cork the bottle and store in a cool, dark place for up to 1 year.

HONEYDEW — AMBROSIA
MELON $4 EA. — SNOW
TUSCAN   MELON
CANTALOUPE

Summer
the Season of Full Growth

Summer is all about abundance. The long, warm days encourage the final cycle of plant growth, producing the thick-fleshed fruiting bodies that characterize the season's favorite vegetables. As a vegetable ripens, the seeds inside grow and begin to mature. Some vegetables are considered at their culinary prime when the seeds are quite immature, as in the case of summer squashes, cucumbers, green beans, and eggplants. For tomatoes, melons, and sweet peppers, however, their prime coincides with the maturation of the seeds at the end of the life cycle. Sweet corn falls midcycle, at its best when the seeds, or kernels, are fully formed but still plump with moisture.

Up and down the state's great Central Valley, from Gridley to Visalia, starting in June, fruit growers bring their sun-ripened crops to market, seducing buyers with purple, red, pink, and green plums and red- or pink-blushed nectarines and peaches that reveal yellow or white flesh when cut open. By August, the melons and watermelons are in the market and baskets of plump figs and bunches of grapes have begun to appear, all to be quickly followed by the first pears and apples.

Summer's market stalls are heaped with the bright reds, golds, and greens of peppers and tomatoes grown in the hot valley climates. From the cooler coastal regions come green beans, celery root, onions, and lettuce.

Cooking is easy now. Nearly everything can go on the outdoor grill—sardines, sweet peppers, eggplants, short ribs, and more—and all of it tastes good with a salad. What could be simpler? As we enjoy the warm days and nights of summer, the chill of fall is not yet on the air.

Fried Padrón Peppers with Goat Cheese and Crostini

In Spain, small, wrinkled bright green padrón peppers are popular served as fried tapas. In recent years, California growers such as Capay Organic, a family farm in the Capay Valley northwest of Sacramento, have been cultivating the peppers, which have made their way onto the menus of many restaurants and tapas bars in the Bay Area and Sacramento Valley. The peppers are mild when small but heat up as they grow larger, so be careful.

12 to 16 thin baguette slices

2 cloves garlic, halved

2 to 3 tablespoons extra-virgin olive oil

12 to 16 padrón peppers with stems intact, 1 to 1½ inches long

½ teaspoon coarse sea or kosher salt

3 to 4 ounces soft fresh goat cheese

1. Preheat the oven to 350°F, prepare a medium-hot fire in a wood or charcoal grill, or preheat a gas grill to medium-high.

2. Arrange the bread slices on a baking sheet and place in the oven or put them on the grill directly over the fire. Cook until golden on the first side, about 5 minutes in the oven or 1 to 2 minutes on the grill, then turn and cook on the second side for about 5 minutes longer in the oven or 1 to 2 minutes on the grill.

3. Transfer the bread slices to a work surface and rub one side of each toasted slice with the garlic. The coarse, crisp surface of the bread will act as a grater.

4. In a frying pan over medium-high heat, warm the olive oil. When it is hot, add the peppers and fry, turning often, until they are slightly collapsed and are lightly charred, about 5 minutes. Using a slotted spoon, transfer to paper towels to drain briefly.

5. Arrange the peppers on a platter and sprinkle with the salt. Accompany with the toasts and the goat cheese. Invite diners to spread the cheese on the toasts and eat along with the fried peppers.

Serves 4

Bruschetta with Ricotta, Dill, and Smoked Salmon

Italian bruschette, toasts with toppings, are one of the easiest appetizers to vary with the seasons. Be sure to slice the bread thinly. That way, the topping is the main flavor, and the bread, often rubbed with garlic, is simply a carrier. We use a baguette here, but other types of artisanal bread will work as well. You can vary the cheese, too, using a soft farmer cheese or soft fresh goat cheese in place of the ricotta. All of these cheeses go well with summer's dill.

12 thin baguette slices

2 cloves garlic, halved

1 tablespoon extra-virgin olive oil

½ to ¾ cup (4 to 6 ounces) whole-milk ricotta cheese

¼ cup finely chopped fresh dill

4 ounces smoked salmon, cut into slivers

1. Preheat the oven to 350°F, prepare a medium-hot fire in a wood or charcoal grill, or preheat a gas grill to medium-high.

2. Arrange the bread slices on a baking sheet and place in the oven or put them on the grill directly over the fire. Cook until golden on the first side, about 5 minutes in the oven or 1 to 2 minutes on the grill, then turn and cook on the second side for about 5 minutes longer in the oven or 1 to 2 minutes on the grill.

3. Transfer the bread slices to a work surface and rub one side of each toasted slice with the garlic. The coarse, crisp surface of the bread will act as a grater. Drizzle the olive oil evenly over the toasts, then spread each toast with an equal amount of the cheese. Scatter the dill evenly over the cheese and arrange the slivers of salmon on top. Arrange on a platter and serve immediately.

Makes 12 toasts; serves 4 to 6

Old-Fashioned Corn Chowder with Rouille

Come summer, the market is filled with wagonloads of fresh corn from all over, but the Brentwood sweet corn, from eastern Contra Costa County, has a strong following. A line often forms for both the white and the yellow corn, and the stock is frequently sold out by midway through the market day, especially at the beginning of corn season, when everyone is eager for the flavor once again. We buy it for grilling, steaming, salads, fricassees, and for chowders, like this one. Keeping the chowder as simple as possible allows the flavor of the corn to dominate. Adding the "milk" from the corn and a few of the cobs increases the corn flavor. Rouille, a spicy Provençal sauce made from chiles, garlic, and olive oil, nicely balances the sweetness of the corn.

Rouille

2 dried cayenne or other hot chiles, seeded

6 to 8 cloves garlic, coarsely chopped

Large pinch of coarse sea or kosher salt

2 large pinches of fresh bread crumbs

½ teaspoon saffron threads soaked in 1 tablespoon hot water

2 egg yolks, at room temperature

½ to ¾ cup extra-virgin olive oil

Chowder

6 ears white or yellow corn, or a mixture, husks and silk removed

2 tablespoons unsalted butter

½ cup minced yellow onion

5 cups whole milk

1 bay leaf

1 fresh rosemary sprig, 6 inches long

½ teaspoon sea or kosher salt

½ teaspoon freshly ground black pepper

12 baguette slices, toasted

1 To make the rouille, in a mortar with a pestle, grind the chiles to a powder. Add the garlic and salt and crush and pound until a paste forms. Add the bread crumbs and the saffron and its soaking water and incorporate into the paste. Scrape the paste into a bowl. Add the egg yolks and whisk until the mixture has thickened. Whisking constantly, slowly add the olive oil, a drop at a time, whisking until the mixture emulsifies and a mayonnaise-like consistency forms. Add only as much of the oil as needed to achieve a good consistency. Cover and refrigerate the rouille until serving.

2 To make the chowder, working with 1 ear of corn at a time, hold the corn, tip down, in a large, wide bowl and, using a sharp knife, cut straight down between the kernels and the cob, cutting as close to the cob as possible without including the fibrous base of the kernels and rotating the ear about a quarter turn after each cut. When all of the kernels have been removed, run the back of the knife along the length of the stripped ear to capture any remaining corn milk in the bowl. Repeat with the remaining ears. Break 2 cobs in half and set aside for the soup. Discard the remaining cobs. Drain the corn kernels in a sieve placed over a bowl and set the milk and kernels aside separately.

3 In a heavy saucepan over medium-high heat, melt the butter. When it foams, add the onion and sauté until soft and nearly translucent, 2 to 3 minutes. Add the corn milk, milk, bay leaf, rosemary, reserved corn cobs, salt, and pepper and bring to just below a boil. Reduce the heat to low and simmer, uncovered, for about 30 minutes to allow the milk to absorb the flavors. Remove and discard the cobs.

4 Add half of the corn kernels and simmer over low heat until just tender, about 5 minutes. Using an immersion blender, coarsely purée the soup. Add the remaining corn kernels and cook just until tender, 4 to 5 minutes.

5 Ladle the soup into warmed bowls. Drizzle each serving with a little of the rouille and serve immediately. Pass the remaining rouille at the table with the toasts.

Serves 4 to 6

Sweet Corn and Fresh Oregano Fritters

Ann and I can sit and eat these fritters by the plateful. Crispy brown, sprinkled with coarse sea salt and fresh oregano, they make a good first course or side dish, or even a main course accompanied with a tomato salad. There is just enough batter to hold the fritters together so the taste of the corn dominates. You can serve these on their own or with a dollop of crème fraîche.

4 ears white or yellow corn, husks and silk removed

¼ yellow onion

1¼ cups all-purpose flour

½ teaspoon baking powder

Coarse sea or kosher salt

¼ teaspoon freshly ground black pepper

3 tablespoons chopped fresh oregano

1 egg, lightly beaten

Extra-virgin olive oil for frying

Crème fraîche for serving (optional)

1. Hold 1 ear of corn, tip down, in a large, wide bowl and, using a sharp knife, cut straight down between the kernels and the cob, cutting as close to the cob as possible without including the fibrous base of the kernels and rotating the ear about a quarter turn after each cut. Repeat with the remaining ear.

2. Using the coarse holes on a box grater, grate the onion. Using your hand, squeeze the onion as dry as you can and then add it to the corn. Sprinkle the flour, baking powder, 1 teaspoon salt, the pepper, and 2 tablespoons of the oregano over the corn and onion mixture and mix well. Add the egg and again mix well.

3. Pour the olive oil to a depth of a scant ¼ inch into a frying pan and heat over medium-high heat. When the oil is hot, form each fritter by dropping the corn mixture by the heaping teaspoonful into the hot oil, spacing them about 1 inch apart. Press down gently with the back of a spatula and fry until golden brown on the first side, about 2 minutes.

4 Turn and fry the second side, about 1 minute. Using a slotted spatula or slotted spoon, transfer the fritters to paper towels to drain. Cook the remaining fritters the same way, adding more oil if needed and reducing the heat if necessary to avoid scorching.

5 Arrange the fritters on a warmed platter and sprinkle with salt and the remaining 1 tablespoon oregano. Top each fritter with a small dollop of crème fraîche, if desired. Serve immediately.

Makes 12 to 16 fritters; serves 4 to 6

Watermelon, Cucumber, and Heirloom Cherry Tomato Salad

When the temperature hits 90 degrees or more, the long-awaited tomatoes start hitting the market. Under the shade of the market's pavilion, shoppers stroll by heirloom cherry tomatoes in a rainbow of colors bearing old-fashioned names like Super Snow White, Aunt Ruby's German Green, and Honkin' Big Black Cherry. The cucumbers, distinct from their supermarket cousins because they are not coated with wax, arrive in early summer. In our summer market salads we like to experiment with the flavors of different cucumber varieties, like the round, yellow Lemon, the long, thin, pale Armenian, and the dark green, curling Serpent. We mix the tomatoes and cucumbers with watermelon to capture a wealth of summer tastes in a single dish.

½ small seedless yellow or red watermelon, rind trimmed and flesh cut into ½-inch cubes (about 3 cups)

3 cucumbers, peeled if the skin is thick or bitter and cut into ½-inch cubes (about 2 cups)

1 pint heirloom green, black, or yellow cherry tomatoes, halved (about 2 cups)

Zest of 1 lime, removed in wide strips

Juice of 1 to 2 limes (about ¼ cup)

Juice of 1 lemon (about ¼ cup)

½ to ¾ teaspoon sea or kosher salt

½ teaspoon pure chile powder such as ancho or New Mexico

1 In a large serving bowl, combine the watermelon, cucumbers, and cherry tomatoes. Chop the lime zest into ¼-inch pieces and add to the salad. Add the lime and lemon juices and toss to coat evenly. Add the salt and chile powder and toss again. Cover and refrigerate for at least 1 hour or up to 3 hours before serving. Serve chilled.

Serves 8 to 10

Grilled Fresh Sardines

From late spring until late summer, sardines are abundant in Monterey Bay and its environs. The O'Shea family, which operates Mission Fresh Fish, pulls the prized silvery fish from those waters and sells them at our market. The fish stall is my first stop during sardine season, because when it has them, they sell out fast. I keep it simple when I serve the fish, grilling them whole and encouraging my guests to pick them up and eat them the way a Marseillaise friend taught me: hold the head in one hand, the tail in the other, and eat down to the bones. Count on four or five fish per diner, more for sardine aficionados like me and Ann.

16 to 20 sardines, about 6 inches long

¼ cup extra-virgin olive oil, plus more for the grill

1 teaspoon coarse sea or kosher salt

½ teaspoon freshly ground black pepper

2 lemons, thinly sliced

1 To clean the fish, make a 1- to 2-inch slit along the belly. With your fingers, reach into the cavity and pull out and discard the entrails. Rinse the cavity and the fish and set aside on paper towels to drain. When all of the fish are cleaned, pat them dry and place in a shallow baking dish. Drizzle with the olive oil, sprinkle with the salt and pepper, and turn several times to coat evenly. Leave to marinate while you prepare the fire.

2 Prepare a medium-hot fire in a wood or charcoal grill or preheat a gas grill to medium-high. When the coals are ready, rub the grill rack with olive oil and place the fish on the rack. Cook until the skin is crisp and golden on the first side, 4 to 5 minutes. Turn and cook on the second side until crisp and golden, 4 to 5 minutes longer. Transfer the sardines to a platter.

3 Place the lemon slices on the grill rack and grill, turning once, until soft and slightly golden on both sides, about 1 minute on each side. Transfer the lemon slices to the platter and serve immediately.

Serves 4

Roast Chicken with 40 Cloves of Garlic

Late June and early July is the best time to make this dish. That's when freshly dug garlic, rather than storage garlic, is available at the market. You can identify fresh garlic by the thick, still-moist stalks and the not-yet-dry skin of the bulb. The cloves are pure white and full of flavor yet mild, and they are the traditional choice for this seasonal dish. The unpeeled cloves and full heads are roasted along with the chicken and then served with toasted bread at the table.

- 1 chicken, 4½ to 5 pounds
- Sea or kosher salt and freshly ground black pepper
- 2 tablespoons chopped mixed fresh rosemary, sage, and thyme
- 2 fresh thyme sprigs
- 2 fresh rosemary sprigs
- 2 fresh sage sprigs
- 2 fresh flat-leaf parsley sprigs
- 40 cloves young garlic, unpeeled, plus 4 to 6 heads
- 3 tablespoons extra-virgin olive oil
- 8 to 10 baguette or coarse country bread slices, toasted or grilled

1 Preheat the oven to 400°F.

2 Gently slip your hand between the skin and breast meat of the chicken to make a pocket. Rub the meat well with salt, pepper, and the chopped herbs and pat the skin back into place. Rub the cavity and the outside of the bird with salt and pepper. Put 1 each of the thyme, rosemary, sage, and parsley sprigs and 4 garlic cloves in the cavity.

3 Put the chicken, breast side up, in a shallow baking pan just large enough to hold it and rub it all over with the olive oil. Add the remaining herb sprigs and garlic cloves and the garlic heads to the pan, tucking them snugly around the chicken.

4 Roast for 15 minutes, then reduce the oven temperature to 375°F and continue to roast until the skin is golden brown and the juices run clear when a thigh joint is pierced with the tip of a knife, 1¼ to 1½ hours.

5 Transfer the chicken to a cutting board and let stand for 5 minutes. Scoop the garlic out of the pan, then strain the pan juices into a clear glass measuring cup, let stand for a few minutes, and skim off the fat to make a jus.

6 Carve the chicken into serving pieces, place them on a platter, and surround them with the garlic. Drizzle the jus over the chicken and serve accompanied with the toasted bread. At the table, invite diners to crush the garlic slightly and then squeeze the soft cloves free of their papery jackets for spreading onto the toasts.

Serves 4–6

Zucchini and Gruyère Gratin

With this recipe, brought home from France by Georgeanne, my family never tires of zucchini in the summer. It's also a great way to use your day-old baguette or other coarse-crumbed bread. The key to the gratin is to use very young squash with virtually no seed development. Many farmers at the market offer a wide selection of young summer squashes, any one of which you can use here.

4 tablespoons extra-virgin olive oil, plus more for the gratin dish

¼ teaspoon coarse sea salt

⅓ cup chopped fresh flat-leaf parsley

4 cloves garlic

2 pounds young, small zucchini, trimmed and very thinly sliced into coins, preferably on a mandoline

Sea or kosher salt and freshly ground black pepper

6 day-old baguette slices, crusts removed

2 cups hot water

4 ounces Gruyère or Emmentaler cheese, cut into ⅛- to ¼-inch dice

2 eggs

1 Preheat the oven to 425°F. Lightly oil a 7-by-12-inch gratin dish.

2 In a mortar with a pestle, crush and pound together the salt, parsley, and garlic until a paste forms. Set aside.

3 In a frying pan over medium-high heat, warm 3 tablespoons of the olive oil. When the oil is hot, add the zucchini slices, sprinkle with a little salt and pepper, and sauté until limp and lightly golden, 15 to 20 minutes. The long sauté removes the moisture from the squash and makes for a firmer gratin. Remove from the heat and reserve.

4 In a bowl, combine the bread and water and let soak until the bread is fully moistened, then squeeze the bread very dry with your hands and discard the water. In a large bowl, combine the bread, cheese, eggs, parsley mixture, and a pinch each of salt and pepper. Beat with a fork until the mixture is fluffy. Add the zucchini and toss to combine evenly with the bread mixture. Spoon the mixture into the prepared gratin dish and sprinkle the surface evenly with the remaining 1 tablespoon olive oil.

5 Bake the gratin until puffed and golden, about 30 minutes. Let cool for about 5 minutes before serving.

Serves 4

Grilled Eggplant Sandwich with Grilled Sweet Peppers and Basil Aioli

Here, aioli, homemade mayonnaise with garlic, includes basil as well, making this summertime sandwich special. In theory, aioli is simple to make, but achieving the proper consistency can sometimes be a challenge. Although it is time-consuming, adding the oil one drop at a time is essential to achieving a good result.

Basil Aioli

3 cloves garlic

½ teaspoon coarse sea salt

8 to 10 fresh basil leaves, finely chopped

2 egg yolks

¾ to 1 cup extra-virgin olive oil or equal parts grape seed or canola oil and extra-virgin olive oil

2 large globe eggplants, sliced crosswise a scant ½ inch thick, or 3 to 4 long eggplants, sliced lengthwise a scant ½ inch thick

Extra-virgin olive oil as needed

Coarse sea salt

3 or 4 good-size sweet peppers of any type and any color, seeded and cut lengthwise into 2-inch-wide strips

4 soft bread rolls, split

1 cup fresh basil leaves (from about 5 large sprigs)

1 To make the aioli, in a mortar with a pestle, crush the garlic with the salt until a paste forms. Add the basil and crush and pound until well combined. Set aside.

2 In a bowl, whisk the egg yolks until they turn a pale yellow, about 5 minutes. Add the olive oil, a drop at a time, while whisking constantly. Keep adding the oil a drop at a time and whisking constantly until the mixture begins to thicken, 8 to 10 minutes. At this point, you

will have added about ½ cup of the oil. Now you can begin adding the oil in a slow, thin, steady stream while continuing to whisk vigorously. When the mixture is the consistency of mayonnaise, you can stop adding oil. Whisk in the garlic mixture until evenly distributed. If the mixture begins to separate, or "break," while you are whisking in the oil, begin again with another egg yolk in a clean bowl, whisk it until it is pale yellow, and then add the broken oil-egg mixture to the new egg yolk, a drop at a time, until the egg yolk thickens. This can be done up to two times if necessary. You should have about ¾ cup aioli. Cover and refrigerate until serving.

3 Prepare a medium-hot fire in a wood or charcoal grill or preheat a gas grill to medium-high.

4 Brush both sides of each eggplant slice with olive oil and then sprinkle both sides lightly with salt. Place the slices on the grill rack directly over the fire and cook until golden brown on the first side, about 5 minutes. Turn and cook on the second side until golden brown and tender, about 5 minutes longer. Transfer to a platter.

5 In a bowl, toss the sweet peppers with about 2 tablespoons olive oil to coat evenly. Add a little salt and toss again. Transfer the pepper strips to a metal grill pan or basket, place directly over the fire, and cook, stirring often if using a grill pan or turning often if using a basket, until lightly browned, about 10 minutes. Transfer to the platter with the eggplant. Just before the peppers come off of the grill, brush the cut sides of the rolls with olive oil and grill, oiled side down, just until golden, about 1 minute.

6 Transfer the rolls, cut sides up, to a work surface. To assemble each sandwich, spread the cut sides of each roll with the aioli. Place 2 or 3 eggplant slices on the bottom half of each roll, followed by several pepper strips and several basil leaves. Close the sandwiches with the roll tops and then cut in half if you like. Arrange the sandwiches on a platter and serve right away.

Makes 4 sandwiches

Planked Salmon

From summer into fall, you'll find locally caught wild salmon at the market, often in large fillets—almost half a fish—with glistening skin and succulent-looking orange flesh. These big fillets lend themselves to cooking on a wooden plank, Pacific Northwest style, which infuses them with a smoky, woodsy flavor.

¼ cup kosher salt

1 large salmon fillet, about 2 pounds, or 2 fillets, about 1 pound each, 1 to 1½ inches thick

2 tablespoons Dijon mustard

1 tablespoon soy sauce

2 tablespoons dark brown sugar

1 teaspoon sea or kosher salt

1 teaspoon freshly ground black pepper

Canola or sunflower oil for the grill rack

1. You will need a cedar plank about 9 by 14 inches and ½ inch thick. Select a container just large enough to hold the plank and pour in enough water to cover the plank by a couple of inches. Add the ¼ cup salt and stir until dissolved. Submerge the plank in the water and let soak for at least 2 hours or up to 3 hours.

2. Build a hot fire in a wood or charcoal grill, or preheat a gas grill to high.

3. Remove the skin from the salmon, if necessary. Run a fingertip lengthwise down the fillet(s) to check for pin bones and use tweezers to remove any you find.

4. Remove the plank from the water. In a bowl, stir together the mustard, soy sauce, brown sugar, 1 teaspoon salt, and pepper to make a paste. Lay the fish, skinned side down, on the plank. Using a brush, coat the top surface of the fish with the mustard paste.

5. When the fire is ready, adjust the heat for indirect grilling: If using a wood or charcoal fire, move the coals evenly to the sides of the grill bed, leaving the center empty. If using a gas grill, turn off one burner. Rub the grill rack with canola oil. Place the plank on the grill rack away from the direct heat. Cover the grill and cook until the salmon flakes to the touch of a fork, about 12 minutes per inch of thickness.

6. Remove the plank from the grill and carefully transfer the salmon to a platter. Serve hot.

Serves 6 to 8

HEIRLOOM TOMATOES

Some of the earliest organic farmers in Yolo County, like Kathy Barsotti and Martin Barnes, cofounders of Capay Organic and the Davis Farmers Market, pioneered the comeback of heirloom tomatoes in the 1980s. These new farmers were developing a market for their products with San Francisco Bay Area restaurants, and not surprisingly, all of the restaurants wanted a tomato with good old-fashioned flavor.

Farmers began asking friends for seeds, and restaurant clients brought back seeds from their travels to Europe. Seed Savers Exchange, a clearinghouse for perpetuating old varieties, became an important seed source as well. All of the seeds came in small quantities, however, often less than a dozen. The intrepid farmers planted and labeled them in trials and then evaluated them, judging them not only for flavor but also for productivity, disease resistance, and suitability to various microclimates. They saved the seeds of the tomatoes that tasted and performed best.

Thanks to the efforts of these and other early market growers, heirloom tomatoes are a staple of the Davis Farmers Market and of farmers' markets nationwide. What exactly are heirloom tomatoes? Various definitions exist, but an heirloom tomato is generally considered to be a variety that has been around for at least fifty years and is open pollinated (the seed produces a fruit identical to its parent). Heirloom tomatoes come in all shapes, sizes, and colors, but above all, they must have outstanding flavor. That is what brings the customers back to the market for tomatoes, and what causes us to long for tomato season and to mourn its passing with the first hard frost in late fall.

Among our favorites are the black varieties, Black Krim and Black Prince, with their rich, slightly musky taste. Cherokee Purple has superb flavor, as do the large—sometimes a pound or more—Marvel Stripe, Brandywine, and Mortgage Lifter. Evergreen, White Wonder, Ponderosa Pink, New Zealand Pink Pear, Green Grape, Green Zebra—the names alone entice us to buy them, but we also know how good they always taste.

ROASTED HEIRLOOM TOMATO SAUCE WITH OLIVES AND HERBS

This sauce has a slightly caramelized flavor, with a hint of tartness from the olives. It is strained so it is an elegant, rather than chunky, sauce, and its color depends on the tomatoes. Most heirlooms available at the market are slicers, which means they have a higher moisture to pulp content than paste tomatoes, like San Marzano. Consequently, it takes longer for the sauce to thicken and you end up with less sauce than if you had started with an equivalent amount of paste tomatoes. However, the flavor more than makes up for the extra cooking time and the smaller yield.

10 to 12 large heirloom tomatoes such as Pink or Yellow Brandywine, Marvel Stripe, or Purple Cherokee (about 5 pounds total)

15 Mediterranean-style black olives, pitted

15 green olives, pitted

1 clove garlic, minced

15 fresh basil leaves, chopped

1 teaspoon fresh thyme leaves

1 teaspoon coriander seeds

1 teaspoon fennel seeds

¼ cup plus 1 tablespoon extra-virgin olive oil

Juice of 1 lemon

¼ cup minced shallots

1½ cups Sauvignon Blanc

1 tablespoon balsamic vinegar

½ to 1 teaspoon sea salt

½ teaspoon freshly ground black pepper

Preheat the oven to 400°F.

Core the tomatoes but leave them whole. Put them in a roasting pan, stacking them if necessary. Sprinkle the black and green olives, garlic, basil, thyme, coriander, and fennel evenly over the tomatoes, then drizzle ¼ cup of the olive oil and the lemon juice over the top.

Roast the tomatoes until they are soft and collapsing, about 40 minutes. Remove from the oven.

In a large saucepan over medium heat, warm the remaining 1 tablespoon olive oil. When it is hot, add the shallots and sauté until translucent, 2 to 3 minutes. Add the tomato mixture and wine and cook over medium heat, stirring, until the tomatoes have thickened and the flavors have blended, about 40 minutes. Remove from the heat and let cool slightly.

Working in batches if necessary, transfer the mixture to a food processor or blender and process until smooth. Strain the purée through a fine-mesh sieve or a chinois to remove the seeds and bits of skin. Taste and adjust the seasoning with salt and pepper if needed. Use immediately, or cover and refrigerate for up to 3 days or freeze for up to 6 months.

Makes about 6 cups

Barbecued Short Ribs with Dark Sauce

Big, wide-cut, meaty short ribs are the kind that Karen and Scott Stone of Yolo Land and Cattle Company sell, and the ribs take readily to a thick barbecue sauce. We cook them in simmering water first, then we marinate them in a sauce, and finally we finish them on the grill to give them that seared, smoky taste.

- 12 beef short ribs (about 3 pounds total)
- 1 tablespoon canola or sunflower oil, plus more for the grill
- 2 tablespoons chopped yellow onion
- 4 cloves garlic, minced
- 1 cup ketchup, homemade (page 133) or purchased
- 2 tablespoons Dijon mustard
- 2 tablespoons dark brown sugar
- 3 tablespoons dry sherry
- 2 tablespoons red wine vinegar
- 1 tablespoon Worcestershire sauce
- 1 teaspoon red pepper flakes
- 1 teaspoon freshly ground black pepper
- Sea or kosher salt

1. Bring a large pot three-fourths full of water to a boil over high heat. Add the ribs, reduce the heat to medium, and simmer uncovered, skimming off any foam that gathers on the surface, until the meat is easily pierced with the tines of a fork and is starting to pull away from the bones, about 1½ hours.

2. Using a wire skimmer, transfer the ribs to a platter and pat dry. Reserve the cooking liquid.

3. In a large saucepan over medium-high heat, warm the oil. When the oil is hot, add the onion and sauté until translucent, 2 to 3 minutes. Stir in the garlic and sauté briefly, then add the ketchup, mustard, brown sugar, sherry, vinegar, Worcestershire sauce, red pepper flakes, and black pepper and mix well. Add several tablespoons of the reserved cooking liquid to make a sauce with the consistency of heavy cream. Taste and adjust the seasoning with salt.

4 Arrange the cooked ribs in a single layer in a shallow baking dish. Pour the sauce over them and turn them several times to coat. Let stand at room temperature for at least 30 minutes or up to 2 hours.

5 Build a hot fire in a wood or charcoal grill or preheat a gas grill to high.

6 When the fire is ready, rub the grill rack with oil. Remove the ribs from the sauce, reserving the sauce. Place the ribs directly over the fire and cook until the first side is well seared and beginning to brown on the edges, about 4 minutes, basting with the reserved sauce. Turn the ribs and cook the same way on the second side, again basting with the sauce.

7 Transfer the ribs to a platter and serve hot.

Serves 4

Braised Okra with Tomatoes and Onion

Ann and I both claim a little southern heritage, so it's not surprising that we like okra, especially the young, tender pods, like those called for here. In this dish, all of the vegetables simmer until the okra pods split, releasing their round, white seeds, and the tomatoes melt and blend with the soft onions. It's not at all like the southern cornmeal-fried classic but it's just as good. I cook this for dinner on summer nights and serve it spooned over a bowl of rice, just like my okra-loving Texas-born mother used to do.

2 tablespoons extra-virgin olive oil

1 yellow onion, thinly sliced

2 cloves garlic, minced

1 pound small okra pods, no more than 1 to 2 inches long

4 tomatoes, cored and coarsely chopped or 4 cups cherry tomatoes, halved

½ teaspoon fresh thyme leaves

½ teaspoon sea or kosher salt

¼ teaspoon freshly ground pepper

1 In a saucepan over medium-high heat, warm the olive oil. When the oil is hot, add the onion and sauté, stirring, until limp, 3 to 4 minutes. Add the garlic and sauté briefly, then add the okra and cook, stirring, until bright green, about 1 minute. Add the tomatoes, thyme, salt, and pepper, reduce the heat to low, cover, and simmer until the onion is soft and the okra pods are tender and have just split, 35 to 40 minutes.

2 Taste and adjust the seasoning with salt and pepper if needed. Transfer to a serving bowl and serve hot or at room temperature.

Serves 4

Old-Fashioned Meringues with Berries

In my grandparents' brown-shingled Berkeley house, the freestanding vintage stove dominated the kitchen. Fresh meringues would emerge from my grandmother's oven to be topped with freshly picked blackberries and raspberries from my granddad's kitchen garden. This is my grandmother's recipe for meringues, slightly modified and not too different from Georgeanne's mother's recipe.

Meringue

4 egg whites, at room temperature

1 cup sugar

1 teaspoon distilled white vinegar

1 teaspoon almond or vanilla extract

¼ teaspoon fine sea salt

2 pints blackberries, raspberries, strawberries, blueberries, or a mixture

Whipped Cream (optional)

2 cups heavy cream

½ teaspoon sugar

½ teaspoon almond or vanilla extract

1 Preheat the oven to 275°F. Line a large rimmed baking sheet with parchment paper.

2 To make the meringue, place the egg whites in a large bowl. Using an electric mixer on low speed, beat the egg whites until frothy, about 1 minute. Increase the speed to medium-high and continue beating until soft peaks form, 2 to 3 minutes. Then add the sugar, 1 tablespoon at a time, and beat until stiff, shiny peaks form, about 5 minutes. Add the vinegar, almond extract, and salt and beat for 1 minute.

3 Using a spoon, transfer the meringue batter to the baking sheet, forming 3-inch rounds about 2 inches high, forming several peaks on each round with the spoon. You should have 10 meringues. If you like, use the back of the spoon to make a slight depression in each meringue, to act as a cup to hold the berries.

4 Bake the meringues until very faint color appears on the peaks, about 1 hour. The outside will be crisp and the inside soft. When they are done, turn off the oven, crack the oven door open, and let the meringues dry out in the oven as it cools, at least 1 hour or up to 6 hours to ensure they are fully dry.

5 If making the whipped cream, pour the cream into a large bowl. Using the electric mixer on medium-high speed, beat until soft peaks form, 3 to 4 minutes. Add the sugar and almond extract and continue to beat until stiff peaks form, 2 to 3 minutes longer.

6 To serve, place each meringue on a dessert plate. Top the meringues with the berries and then with a scoop of the whipped cream, if using.

Makes 10 meringues; serves 10

Roasted Summer Fruits with Ice Cream

This is by far the easiest summer and early fall dessert I know, and when I serve it, people never fail to marvel, including Ann. Imagine fruit cobbler, but without the crust. During summer and into fall, the market is brimming with dozens of varieties of stone fruits, and as late summer comes, with figs and grapes as well.

8 to 12 stone fruits, such as peaches, plums, nectarines, or Pluots; figs; and grape clusters, in any combination

1 to 2 tablespoons extra-virgin olive oil

½ to ¾ cup sugar

Vanilla ice cream for serving

1 Preheat the oven to 450°F.

2 Halve and pit the stone fruits. Leave the figs whole. Separate the grapes into small clusters of 3 or 4 grapes, or separate them into single grapes. Place the fruits in a baking dish in which they will nudge together in roughly a layer and a half and drizzle them with the olive oil. Turn the fruits several times, sprinkle them with the sugar, and turn again.

3 Roast the fruits until they are tender and slightly caramelized on top and a syrup has formed, 15 to 20 minutes. Remove from the oven and spoon into dessert bowls. Add a scoop of ice cream to each bowl and serve warm.

Serves 4 to 6

Plum Jam

Fruit growers typically grow multiple varieties of single fruits, including plums, in order to have enough to sell throughout the summer. Each plum variety makes a slightly differently flavored and colored jam. Pectin, which is necessary for jam to jell, occurs naturally in fruits in varying degrees. Underipe fruits generally have more pectin, and sometimes jam makers throw in a single immature fruit just for the pectin content. Like citrus fruits, blackberries, and apples, plums are naturally high in pectin, so we don't add any to our plum jam.

You will need three pint canning jars with lids and rings, a large canning kettle with a rack and cover (or a large, wide pot with a wire rack and cover) for the water bath, a large, heavy nonreactive pot for cooking the jam, canning tongs, and a ladle.

3 pounds plums, any variety, pitted and chopped (about 6 cups)

½ cup fresh lemon juice

4 cups sugar, or as needed

1 Taste a piece of plum to see if the batch is sweet or tart. Place the plums in the large, heavy nonreactive pot. Add the lemon juice and then add 4 cups sugar if the plums are sweet or slightly more if they are tart. Stir gently and set aside for 1 hour to bring the juice out of the plums.

2 To set up the water bath, fill the canning kettle with water (the water must be deep enough to cover the jars by 1 to 2 inches) and bring to a boil over high heat. If you don't have a canning kettle, use a large, wide pot and put a wire rack in the bottom of the pot before you fill it with water. Once the water boils, you can turn off the heat and then return it to a boil just before you put the jars in the kettle.

3 Meanwhile, wash the canning jars in hot, soapy water and rinse well. Place the jars in a large saucepan, add water to cover generously, and bring to a boil over medium-high heat. Boil for 15 minutes, then turn off the heat and leave the jars in the hot water until you are ready to fill them. Fill another saucepan half full with water and bring to a boil over medium-high heat. Add the canning lids and rings and boil for 5 minutes. Turn off the heat and leave the lids and rings in the hot water until needed. Place two or three small saucers in the freezer.

4 When the plums have sat for an hour, place the pot over high heat and bring to a boil. Skim off any foam that forms on top. Continue boiling, stirring continuously, for 10 minutes. Remove from the heat and quickly skim off any additional foam. Test the jam for jelling by placing a teaspoon of it on a chilled saucer. If it develops a skin after 1 minute, it is ready to jell. If not, return the jam to the heat, boil for 5 minutes longer, and retest.

5 Just before the jam is ready, using tongs, transfer the jars to a work surface. Return the water in the canning kettle to a boil. Ladle the hot jam into hot, sterilized jars, filling them to within $1/2$ inch of the rim. With a clean, damp cloth, wipe the rim of each jar. Place a lid on the rim and screw on a ring, being sure not to screw it on too tightly. Put the filled jars into the rack of the canner and lower the rack into the boiling water. If you are using a large, wide pot, use the canning tongs to lower the jars onto the rack in the bottom of the pot, making sure the jars do not touch. Return the water to a rolling boil, reduce the heat slightly, cover, and boil for 5 minutes.

6 Cover a work surface with a folded towel. Using the canning tongs, transfer the jars to the towel, spacing them a few inches apart. As the jars begin to cool, you may hear popping sounds, which is the sound of the lids sealing. The lids should be indented. When the jars are completely cool, after at least 12 hours, check the seal on each jar by pressing on the center of the lid. If it remains indented, the seal is good. If it does not, refrigerate the jar and use the jam within 1 month.

7 Label the jars with the contents and date and store in a cool, dry place for up to 1 year.

Makes 3 pints

Pickled Peaches

As a child, I made these with my grandmother, using the peaches she grew in her backyard orchard in El Monte, California. Like the peaches at the market, they came in all colors and sizes, but the ones we pickled were the yellow ones, the same kind I pickle today. Firm clingstone peaches are best for canning, but firm freestone peaches can be used. Be careful not to overcook the fruit. I serve the peaches as a condiment at Thanksgiving. Ann, after tasting them, has added this recipe to her collection.

You will need two quart canning jars with lids and rings, a large canning kettle with a rack and cover (or a large, wide pot with a wire rack and cover) for the water bath, a large, heavy saucepan for cooking the peaches, a large saucepan for blanching the peaches (optional), canning tongs, and a ladle.

2 cups cider vinegar

2 cups sugar

6 cinnamon sticks, about 2 inches long

12 to 16 medium-size firm peaches, preferably clingstone

Whole cloves, 4 or 5 per peach

1 To set up the water bath, fill the canning kettle with water (the water must be deep enough to cover the jars by 1 to 2 inches) and bring to a boil over high heat. If you don't have a canning kettle, use a large, wide pot and put a wire rack in the bottom of the pot before you fill it with water. Once the water boils, you can turn off the heat and then return it to a boil just before you are ready to put the jars in the kettle.

2 Meanwhile, wash the canning jars in hot, soapy water and rinse well. Place the jars in a large saucepan, add water to cover generously, and bring to a boil over medium-high heat. Boil for 15 minutes, then turn off the heat and leave the jars in the hot water until you are ready to fill them. Fill another saucepan half full with water and bring to a boil over medium-high heat. Add the canning lids and rings and boil for 5 minutes. Turn off the heat and leave the lids and rings in the hot water until needed.

3 In a large saucepan over medium-high heat, combine the vinegar, sugar, and cinnamon and bring to a boil, stirring until the sugar dissolves. Meanwhile, with a paring knife, peel the peaches. Alternatively, fill a large saucepan three-fourths full with water and bring to a boil over high heat. Have ready a large bowl filled with ice water. In batches, add the peaches to the boiling water and leave for 30 seconds to loosen the skin, then scoop them out, plunge them into the ice water until cool, and slip off the skins. Stick each peach with 4 or 5 cloves and immerse the peaches in the boiling syrup. Cook, turning gently with a wooden spoon so as not to damage the fruit, until just tender, about 5 minutes. They will continue to cook in the canning kettle.

4 Once you have added the peaches to the syrup, using tongs, transfer the jars to a work surface. Return the water in the canning kettle to a boil. When the peaches are ready, using a slotted spoon, transfer them to the hot, sterilized jars, then ladle in the syrup, filling the jars to within $1/2$ inch of the rim. With a clean, damp cloth, wipe the rim of each jar. Place a lid on the rim and then screw on a ring, being careful not to screw it on too tightly. Put the filled jars into the rack of the canner and lower the rack into the boiling water. If you are using a large, wide pot, use the canning tongs to lower the jars onto the rack in the bottom of the pot, making sure the jars do not touch. Return the water to a rolling boil, reduce the heat slightly, cover, and boil for 20 minutes.

5 Cover a work surface with a folded towel. Using the canning tongs, transfer the jars to the towel, spacing them a few inches apart. As the jars begin to cool, you may hear popping sounds, which is the sound of the lids sealing. The lids should be indented. When the jars are completely cool, after at least 12 hours, check the seal on each jar by pressing on the center of the lid. If it remains indented, the seal is good. If it does not, refrigerate the jar and use the peaches within 1 month.

6 Label the jars with the contents and date and store in a cool, dry place for up to 1 year.

Makes 2 quarts

Homemade Ketchup

I dedicate a day to ketchup each summer, harvesting some of Georgeanne's tomatoes, which her husband grows in quantity. I triple this recipe to make 12 pints and simmer it all day. If you are making a single recipe, 1 to 2 hours of simmering is adequate. Once you've made your own ketchup, you'll find it hard to return to store-bought.

You will need four pint canning jars with lids and rings, a large canning kettle with a rack and cover (or a large, wide pot with a wire rack and cover) for the water bath, a large, nonreactive pot for cooking the ketchup, a large saucepan for blanching the tomatoes, canning tongs, and a ladle.

10 large, very ripe red tomatoes or a combination of different colors and varieties (about 5 pounds)

2 large yellow or red sweet peppers (about 1½ pounds), seeded and coarsely chopped

2 yellow onions (about 10 ounces each), coarsely chopped

10 cloves garlic, coarsely chopped

1 cup white wine vinegar

Grated zest and juice of ¼ lemon

¾ cup sugar

1½ teaspoons salt

2 teaspoons mustard seeds

1 tablespoon black peppercorns

1 tablespoon coriander seeds

1 teaspoon whole cloves

1-inch piece cinnamon stick

1-inch piece fresh ginger, cut into 3 or 4 pieces

1 Fill a large saucepan three-fourths full with water and bring to a boil over high heat. Have ready a large bowl of ice water. In batches, add the tomatoes to the boiling water and leave for 1 minute to loosen the skins, then scoop them out and plunge them into the ice water. With a paring knife, peel away the skins and cut out the cores. Cut the tomatoes in half crosswise and squeeze each half gently to remove the seeds, using your fingertip to dislodge any seed sacs that do not fall out easily.

2. In the large, nonreactive pot over medium heat, combine the tomatoes, sweet peppers, onions, garlic, ½ cup of the vinegar, and the lemon zest and juice and cook, stirring frequently, until the vegetables are cooked through and soft, 15 to 20 minutes. Remove from the heat and let cool slightly.

3. Working in batches, transfer the vegetable mixture to a blender or food processor and process until coarsely puréed. Return the purée to the pot and add the sugar, salt, and the remaining ½ cup vinegar. In the center of an 8-inch square of triple-layered cheesecloth, combine the mustard seeds, peppercorns, coriander seeds, cloves, cinnamon stick, and ginger. Gather up the corners and tie them with cotton string to make a spice bag. Add the bag to the pot holding the purée.

4. Return the pot to low heat, bring the mixture to a simmer, and cook, stirring occasionally, until it thickens, 1 to 2 hours. Watch carefully so it does not burn. The finished ketchup will be slightly thinner than most commercial ketchups.

5. While the ketchup is simmering, set up the water bath. Fill the canning kettle with water (the water must be deep enough to cover the jars by 1 to 2 inches) and bring to a boil over high heat. If you don't have a canning kettle, use a large, wide pot and put a wire rack in the bottom of the pot before you fill it with water. Once the water boils, you can turn off the heat and then return the water to a boil just before you are ready to put the jars in the kettle.

6. Wash the canning jars in hot, soapy water and rinse well. Place the jars in a saucepan, add water to cover generously, and bring to a boil over medium-high heat. Boil for 15 minutes, then turn off the heat and leave the jars in the hot water until you are ready to fill them. Fill another saucepan half full with water and bring to a boil over medium-high heat. Add the canning lids and rings and boil for 5 minutes. Turn off the heat and leave the lids and rings in the hot water until needed.

7. Just before the ketchup is ready, using tongs, transfer the jars to a work surface. Return the water in the canning kettle to a boil. Ladle the hot ketchup into the hot, sterilized jars, filling them to within ½ inch of the rim. With a clean, damp cloth, wipe the rim of each jar. Place a lid on the rim and then screw on a ring, being careful not to screw it on too tightly. Put the filled canning jars into the rack of the canner and lower the rack into the

boiling water. If you are using a large, wide pot, use the canning tongs to lower the jars onto the rack in the bottom of the pot, making sure the jars do not touch. Return the water to a rolling boil, reduce the heat slightly, cover, and boil for 10 minutes.

8 Cover a work surface with a folded towel. Using the canning tongs, transfer the jars to the towel, spacing them a few inches apart. As the jars begin to cool, you may hear popping sounds, which is the sound of the lids sealing. The lids should be indented. When the jars are completely cool, after at least 12 hours, check the seal on each jar by pressing on the center of the lid. If it remains indented, the seal is good. If it does not, refrigerate the jar and use the ketchup within 1 month.

9 Label the jars with the contents and date and store in a cool, dry place for up to 1 year.

Makes 4 pints

SONG VUE OF VUE FAMILY FARM AT THE MARKET.

Summer Tomato Sauce

A basic tomato sauce is a pantry staple that can be used year-round to sauce pasta and polenta, to add to soups and stews, or as the base for a meat sauce. Georgeanne has many tomato sauce recipes that she has developed over the years and used in her cookbooks and food articles, but we decided that I would develop one especially for this book.

This recipe can be doubled, tripled, quadrupled, or not, depending on how many tomatoes you are canning and how long you want to spend in the kitchen. The sauce can be chunky, a smooth purée, with skin or without, and seasoned with a variety of different ingredients, including a mix of herbs, onions, mushrooms, olives, and wine. I make both a roasted and a stove-top sauce, but always with a Mediterranean flavor profile. My favorite kitchen tool to use here is my traditional French food mill, which purées the sauce while removing the skins. Using a food processor or blender is faster, but it leaves bits of skin.

You will need six pint or three quart canning jars with lids and rings, a large canning kettle with a rack and cover (or a large, wide pot with a wire rack and cover) for the water bath, a food mill or food processor, a large, nonreactive pot or a large roasting pan for cooking the sauce, a large saucepan for blanching the tomatoes (optional), canning tongs, and a ladle.

If you are using a food mill, you do not need to peel the tomatoes. If you are not using a mill, you can remove the skins or not, as you like. To peel them, fill a large saucepan three-fourths full with water and bring to a boil over high heat. Have ready a large bowl of ice water. In batches, add the tomatoes to the boiling water and leave for 1 minute to loosen the skins, then scoop them out and plunge them into the ice water. With a paring knife, peel away the skins, cut out the cores, and quarter the tomatoes. If you are not peeling the tomatoes, core and quarter them.

10 pounds tomatoes	2 tablespoons fresh thyme leaves
½ cup extra-virgin olive oil	2 bay leaves
6 large cloves garlic, coarsely chopped	Sea salt and freshly ground pepper
Leaves from 5 large fresh basil sprigs	6 tablespoons bottled lemon juice
2 tablespoons fresh rosemary leaves	

1 To cook the sauce on the stove top, in the large, nonreactive pot over low heat, combine the tomatoes, olive oil, garlic, basil, rosemary, thyme, and bay leaves and season with salt and pepper. Stir well, cover, and cook until the mixture is simmering, 20 to 25 minutes. Uncover and continue to simmer, stirring frequently, until the sauce has thickened, 1½ to 2 hours. Remove from the heat and remove and discard the bay leaves.

2 To roast the sauce, preheat the oven to 500°F. Put all of the ingredients except for the lemon juice in a roasting pan, place in the oven, and roast, stirring frequently to prevent burning, until the tomatoes have collapsed and thickened into a sauce, 1 to 2 hours. Remove from the oven and remove and discard the bay leaves. If you have roasted the tomatoes with the skin intact, some of the skin will have caramelized, yielding a sweeter sauce.

3 To purée the sauce and remove the skins, pass the stove-top or roasted sauce through the coarse disk of a food mill. Alternatively, purée the sauce in a blender or food processor and then, if you like, pass it through a chinois or a fine-mesh sieve. Otherwise, leave the skins in the sauce.

4 While the tomato sauce is cooking, set up the water bath. Fill the canning kettle with water (the water must be deep enough to cover the jars by 1 to 2 inches) and bring to a boil over high heat. If you don't have a canning kettle, use a large, wide pot and put a wire rack in the bottom of the pot before you fill it with water. Once the water boils, you can turn off the heat and then return the water to a boil just before you are ready to put the jars in the kettle.

5 Wash the canning jars in hot, soapy water and rinse well. Place the jars in a saucepan, add water to cover generously, and bring to a boil over medium-high heat. Boil for 15 minutes, then turn off the heat and leave the jars in the hot water until you are ready to fill them. Fill another saucepan half full with water and bring to a boil over medium-high heat. Add the canning lids and rings and boil for 5 minutes. Turn off the heat and leave the lids and rings in the hot water until needed.

6 Just before the sauce is ready, using tongs, transfer the jars to a work surface. Return the water in the canning kettle to a boil. Ladle the hot sauce into the hot, sterilized jars, filling them to within 1/2 inch of the rim. Add 1 tablespoon of the lemon juice to each pint jar or 2 tablespoons to each quart jar to ensure adequate acidity. With a clean, damp cloth, wipe the rim of each jar. Place a lid on the rim and then screw on a ring, being careful not to screw it on too tightly. Put the filled canning jars into the rack of the canner and lower the rack into the boiling water. If you are using a large, wide pot, use the canning tongs to lower the jars onto the rack in the bottom of the pot, making sure the jars do not touch. Return the water to a rolling boil, reduce the heat slightly, cover, and boil for 30 minutes for pint jars and 45 minutes for quart jars.

7 Cover a work surface with a folded towel. Using the canning tongs, transfer the jars to the towel, spacing them a few inches apart. As the jars begin to cool, you may hear popping sounds, which is the sound of the lids sealing. The lids should be indented. When the jars are completely cool, after at least 12 hours, check the seal on each jar by pressing on the center of the lid. If it remains indented, the seal is good. If it does not, refrigerate the jar and use the sauce within 1 month.

8 Label the jars with the contents and date and store in a cool, dry place for up to 1 year.

Makes 6 pints or 3 quarts

Dill Pickles

My mother lived in Kansas while I was in college and a Kansan farmer's wife gave her this recipe. I've been making these pickles ever since, using the traditional grape leaves for crispness as she did, but also adding alum, the more contemporary agent for crispness. Georgeanne's husband makes dills, too, cutting them into long, thin slices on a mandoline, and we often debate the merits of sliced or unsliced as we trade back and forth. Neither of our pickles is the fermented type, which is an altogether different process.

You will need seven quart canning jars with lids and rings, a large canning kettle with a rack and cover (or a large, wide pot with a wire rack and cover) for the water bath, canning tongs, and a ladle.

- 20 to 25 cucumbers, 4 inches long
- About 1 teaspoon powdered alum
- 6 or 7 cloves garlic, peeled but left whole
- 6 or 7 fresh dill heads
- 6 to 7 fresh hot red chiles such as cherry or serrano
- 6 or 7 fresh grape leaves
- 4 cups cider vinegar
- 1 cup pickling salt
- 3 quarts water

1 Put the cucumbers in a large bowl of cold water to cover and let stand overnight.

2 The next day, set up the water bath. Fill the canning kettle with water (the water must be deep enough to cover the jars by 1 to 2 inches) and bring to a boil over high heat. If you don't have a canning kettle, use a large, wide pot and put a wire rack in the bottom of the pot before you fill it with water. Once the water boils, you can turn off the heat and then return it to a boil just before you put the jars in the kettle.

3 Wash the canning jars in hot, soapy water and rinse well. Place the jars in a saucepan, add water to cover generously, and bring to a boil over medium-high heat. Boil for 15 minutes, then turn off the heat and leave the jars in the hot water until you are ready to fill them. Fill another saucepan half full with water and bring to a boil over medium-high heat. Add

4. the canning lids and rings and boil for 5 minutes. Turn off the heat and leave the lids and rings in the hot water until needed.

4. Using tongs, transfer the jars to a work surface. Cut off the blossom end of each cucumber and pack the cucumbers into the hot, sterilized quart jars. You may not need all of the jars. Add $1/8$ teaspoon powdered alum, 1 clove garlic, 1 dill head, 1 chile, and 1 grape leaf to each jar.

5. Return the water in the canning kettle to a boil. To make the brine, in a large saucepan or stockpot over medium heat, combine the vinegar, pickling salt, and water and bring to a boil, stirring to dissolve the salt. Ladle the hot brine into the jars, filling them to within $1/2$ inch of the rim. Place a lid on each rim and then screw on a ring, being careful not to screw it on too tightly. Put the filled jars into the rack of the canner and lower the rack into the boiling water of the canning kettle. If you are using a large, wide pot, use the canning tongs to lower the jars onto the rack in the bottom of the pot, making sure the jars do not touch. Return the water to a rolling boil, reduce the heat slightly, and boil for 15 minutes.

6. Cover a work surface with a folded towel. Using the canning tongs, transfer the jars to the towel, spacing them a few inches apart. As the jars begin to cool, you may hear popping sounds, which is the sound of the lids sealing. The lids should be indented. When the jars are completely cool, after at least 12 hours, check the seal on each jar by pressing on the center of the lid. If it remains indented, the seal is good. If it does not, refrigerate the jar and use the pickles within 1 month.

7. Label the jars with the contents and date and store in a cool, dry place for up to 1 year. Allow 3 weeks for the flavors to develop before serving.

Makes 6 or 7 quarts

Fall
the Crossover Season

The first days of fall are warm enough for the last of the summer fruits and vegetables to mature, yet cool enough to encourage leafy plant growth and the development of early roots. Plants grown from seeds sowed in late spring and early summer are yielding their fruits, and late-season summer fruits and vegetables are at their sweetest. Figs are now in their second flush at the same time as short-season lettuce, and the early winter-hardy crop of escarole, radicchio, frisée, kale, and collards are just starting to appear in the market, as are the brassicas.

The colors of the market stalls reflect the crossover season, with bright orange persimmons and red pomegranates keeping company with tomatoes and peppers of the same colors, and lettuce, chard, kale, and chicories cohabiting in shades from chartreuse to slate green and magenta. Mushrooms, always in supply at the market, are now supplemented by foraged wild porcini, golden chanterelles, and black *trompettes de la mort*. Early leeks, with their slender white bulbs and vibrant green stalks, are lined up with dark bunches of beets and the first of the hard squashes. Bok choy and choy sum, along with early spinach, are stacked high. Stone fruits have given way to quinces, pears, apples, and the last of the grapes. New crops of local walnuts, almonds, and pistachios are in and at their freshest.

All of this variety and abundance, and the shortening days, turns a cook's attention to slow braises and roasts, though grilling is not yet totally abandoned. In cooking, as in nature, fall is the crossover season, a brief time when we can still enjoy cooking outside, yet look to the cozy kitchen warmth of dishes cooked in the oven.

Grilled Persimmon Crostini with Farmer Cheese

Grilling the Fuyu persimmon gives it a sweet, caramelized flavor that pairs well with tangy, soft farmer cheese, made from cow's milk, or fresh goat cheese. The other popular persimmon we see in fall, the Hachiya, is eaten when soft and almost jellylike, which makes it unsuitable for grilling but perfect for baking, as in Georgeanne's Persimmon Flan on page 173. We serve these grilled toasts throughout the year, topping them with different fruits, according to the seasons. In winter, try them with sliced roasted kumquats; in spring, with roasted chopped strawberries; and in summer, with any of the stone fruits.

4 Fuyu persimmons

2 tablespoons extra-virgin olive oil, plus more for brushing

4 to 5 ounces farmer cheese or soft fresh goat cheese, at room temperature

24 baguette slices, cut on the diagonal about ⅜ inch thick

Fresh thyme leaves for garnish

1. Prepare a medium-hot fire in a wood or charcoal grill or preheat a gas grill to medium-high.

2. Working with 1 persimmon at a time, cut away the stem, then cut in half through the stem end. Cut each half lengthwise into 3 slices and discard any seeds. You should have 24 slices total. Place the slices in a single layer in a shallow dish, drizzle with the olive oil, and turn the slices to coat on both sides. Set aside.

3. In a bowl, using a fork, mash the cheese so it is soft and spreadable. Set aside.

4. Lightly brush both sides of each baguette slice with olive oil. Place the slices directly over the fire and grill until golden on the first side, 1 to 2 minutes. Turn and grill on the second side until golden, 1 to 2 minutes longer. Transfer the toasts to a work surface.

5. Arrange the persimmon slices directly over the fire and grill, turning once, until the flesh starts to glisten and lightly char, 1 to 1½ minutes on each side.

6 Alternatively, preheat the oven to 350°F, brush the baguette slices with olive oil as directed, arrange on a large baking sheet, and toast in the oven, turning once, until golden on both sides, about 5 minutes on each side. Raise the oven temperature to 450°F, arrange the persimmon slices in a baking dish, and roast in the oven, turning several times, until the flesh is shiny and starts to color, 4 to 5 minutes total.

7 Spread each toast with about 2 teaspoons of the cheese and top with a grilled persimmon slice. Garnish each crostino with a few thyme leaves. Serve at once.

Makes 24 crostini; serves 8 to 10

Grilled Fig and Lardon Kebabs

For this bite-size savory-sweet starter, I use my homemade pancetta (page 192) for the lardons. When Georgeanne runs out of pancetta, she buys a slab of bacon at the market, takes it home, and cuts it into stocky 1½-inch-long lardons. Figs arrive in the market in shades of crimson, green, purple, and cream, but the most important thing is that they be fully ripe, indicated by softness and a bent neck or stem. If a fig is firm to the touch, it isn't ripe yet, so its sugars are not fully developed.

16 fresh figs

2 tablespoons extra-virgin olive oil

5-ounce piece pancetta or slab bacon, cut into 16 strips 1½ inches long by ½ inch wide and thick

Canola or other vegetable oil for the grill rack

Fig leaves (optional)

1 If using wooden skewers, soak 16 skewers in water to cover for 30 minutes. Prepare a medium-hot fire in a wood or charcoal grill or preheat a gas grill to medium-high.

2 Arrange the figs in a single layer in a shallow dish, drizzle evenly with the olive oil, and turn gently to coat evenly.

3 Thread 1 lardon lengthwise onto a skewer and push it toward the top. Then thread a fig through the blossom end onto the skewer and again push it toward the top, to leave a long handle. Repeat to assemble 16 skewers total.

4 When the fire is ready, rub the grill rack with the canola oil. Place the skewers directly over the fire and grill, turning once or twice, until the skins of the figs start to glisten and lightly char and the lardon is nicely browned on the outside, 3 to 5 minutes total.

5 Line a platter with fig leaves (if using). Place the kebabs on the platter and serve hot or warm. Or, remove the figs and lardons from the skewers and, when cool enough to handle, slit each fig open and stuff it with a lardon. Arrange on the platter and serve warm.

Makes 16 skewers; serves 6 to 8

Classic Soupe au Pistou with Fresh Shelling Beans

This is the classic late-summer and fall vegetable soup of Provence, and Ann and I have enjoyed it there for many years. In California, we make it with the fresh shelling beans that show up at Mario Busalacchi's of Busalacchi Farms market stall for only a brief period from late August through September. The soup, laced with an unctuous purée of garlic, basil, and olive oil—the pistou—and served hot with lots of crusty baguette or pain au levain slices, makes a hearty one-dish meal.

Pistou

3 or 4 cloves garlic, coarsely chopped

¼ teaspoon coarse sea or kosher salt

1 cup firmly packed fresh basil leaves

⅓ cup extra-virgin olive oil

Soup

1 tablespoon extra-virgin olive oil

1 small yellow onion, diced

1 carrot, peeled and diced

3 small potatoes, peeled and diced

2 medium zucchini, trimmed and diced

1 pound fresh cranberry beans, shelled

1 pound fresh butter or other shelling beans, shelled

2 cups vegetable stock or chicken stock, homemade (page 48) or purchased

4 cups water

1 to 2 teaspoons sea or kosher salt

4 fresh thyme sprigs

4 fresh flat-leaf parsley sprigs

8 ounces young, slender green beans, trimmed and cut into 1-inch lengths

½ cup broken spaghetti pieces (about 1 inch long)

1. To make the pistou, in a mortar with a pestle, crush together the garlic and salt until a paste forms. (Alternatively, use a bowl and pestle.) Add the basil leaves, a little at a time, crushing and pounding well after each addition. Finally, add the olive oil in a thin stream, continuing to mix with the pestle until the mixture has thickened and is an even green. Set aside.

2. To make the soup, in a large saucepan or soup pot over medium-high heat, warm the olive oil. When it is hot, add the onion and sauté until translucent, 2 to 3 minutes. Add the carrot, potatoes, zucchini, and shelling beans and stir several times. Add the stock, water, salt, thyme, and parsley and bring to a boil. Reduce the heat to medium, cover, and cook until all of the vegetables are nearly tender, 4 to 5 minutes. Add the green beans and spaghetti and cook until the spaghetti is tender, 8 to 10 minutes longer.

3. Remove the thyme and parsley sprigs and discard. Taste for salt, adding more if needed. With the back of a fork, crush some of the potatoes and other vegetables to thicken the soup. Stir 1 tablespoon of the soup broth into the pistou. Transfer the soup to a warmed tureen or serving bowl and stir in 2 tablespoons of the pistou. Serve the soup piping hot. Pass the remaining pistou at the table.

Serves 6

Roasted Beet Salad with Fresh Cheese, Toasted Pistachios, and Pistachio Oil

The sweet, earthy taste of freshly harvested beets, roasted until their edges begin to caramelize, combined with the subtle yet sharp tang of fresh goat cheese and the distinctive essence of pistachios creates a simple yet delicious salad. Beet varieties are plentiful in the market, any of which would be good here, and our neighbor, La Tourangelle in nearby Woodland, produces a fine artisanal pistachio oil from locally grown nuts.

6 beets with greens

2 tablespoons extra-virgin olive oil

½ teaspoon coarse sea or kosher salt

12 to 15 young arugula leaves

3 to 4 ounces soft fresh goat cheese

¼ cup pistachio nuts, toasted and coarsely chopped

3 tablespoons pistachio oil

Coarse sea salt to finish

1. Preheat the oven to 350°F.

2. Trim off the greens and the roots from the beets. Trim the leaves, reserving a few of the smallest leaves to use in the salad. Reserve the larger leaves for another use. Quarter the beets through the stem end, then halve each quarter. Select a baking dish just large enough to hold the beet pieces snugly in a single layer and arrange the beets in the dish. Drizzle them with the olive oil and sprinkle with the salt.

3. Roast the beets, turning them several times, until they are tender when pierced with a fork and crisped a bit on the edges, 45 minutes to 1 hour. Let cool to room temperature.

4. Arrange the arugula and reserved small beet leaves on individual plates, dividing them evenly. Divide the cooled beets evenly among the plates and crumble the goat cheese over the top. Scatter the nuts across the salads, then drizzle each salad with a generous ½ tablespoon of the pistachio oil. Finish with a sprinkle of coarse salt and serve at once.

Serves 4

Frisée Salad with Egg and Pancetta

Jim Eldon's farm, Fiddler's Green, produces large heads of frisée with broad hearts of tender blanched leaves that start appearing in the market in early fall and continue into early spring. I buy his frisée to make the sturdy base for this "market lunch" salad my mother and I often enjoy after our customary visit to the Saturday-morning market. I always make mine with two eggs and my homemade pancetta. Georgeanne uses the frisée from Fiddler's Green as the base for a classic salad of warm baked goat cheese.

5 ounces pancetta or 8 ounces bacon, cut into bite-size pieces

1 tablespoon distilled white vinegar

½ teaspoon sea or kosher salt

3 or 6 eggs, depending if 1 or 2 eggs per person

½ large head frisée, primarily the pale inner leaves, torn into bite-size pieces (about 4 cups)

Dressing

⅓ cup extra-virgin olive oil

3 tablespoons red wine vinegar

⅛ teaspoon sea or kosher salt

¼ teaspoon freshly ground black pepper

½ teaspoon Dijon mustard

1 Preheat the oven to 350°F.

2 In a small frying pan over medium heat, fry the pancetta, turning the pieces often, until crisp and golden, 3 to 4 minutes. Using a slotted spoon, transfer to paper towels to drain.

3 Pour water to a depth of 4 inches into a wide saucepan or a deep sauté pan, bring to a boil over medium heat, and add the vinegar and salt. Reduce the heat to medium-low so the water is at a gentle simmer. Crack each egg into a ramekin or small bowl. One at a time, and working quickly, submerge each ramekin about ½ inch into the water and tip the raw egg into the simmering water. Set a timer for 3 minutes exactly. After 1 minute, reduce the heat to low.

4 Meanwhile, make the dressing. In the bottom of a salad bowl, combine the olive oil, vinegar, salt, and pepper and mix well. Stir in the mustard, mixing well. Add the frisée but do not toss.

5 When the eggs are almost done, toss the salad and divide among individual plates. Divide the pancetta among the plates. When the eggs are done, remove the pan from the heat. With a slotted spoon, lift each egg from the water, pat the bottom briefly on a paper towel to absorb the excess moisture, and then place in the center the salad. Serve immediately.

Serves 3

Salad of Early Bitter Greens and Late Cherry Tomatoes

It's hard to say which I like better, the bitter members of the chicory family, like escarole, frisée, and radicchio, or sweet tomatoes. It is only in late September and early October, when both are found at the market, that I can enjoy them together. At home, I always plant several long rows of the chicories that I share with Ann and others, but they're not ready for harvest until after my tomatoes are gone, so I buy the tomatoes at the market.

¼ cup extra-virgin olive oil

1 tablespoon minced shallot

2 tablespoons Champagne vinegar

¼ teaspoon sea or kosher salt

¼ teaspoon freshly ground black pepper

10 to 15 cherry tomatoes, halved

1 head escarole, pale inner yellow leaves only, torn into bite-size pieces

1 cup fresh flat-leaf parsley leaves

1 cup baby arugula leaves

½ cup cut-up fresh chives, about ½-inch lengths

1 In the bottom of a salad bowl, combine the olive oil, shallots, vinegar, salt, and pepper and mix well. Add the tomatoes and stir, crushing some of the tomatoes to release their juice. Add the escarole, parsley, arugula, and chives. Toss just before serving.

Serves 4

Grilled Stuffed Squid

Monterey Bay is the source for our local squid, and stuffing then grilling them is a change from deep-frying them in batter, though I do love them prepared that way as well. It does take time to clean and stuff them, but the end result is quite impressive. Instead of the fennel seeds, pork, and garlic below, you can substitute Ann's homemade sausage (see page 158). Serving them accompanied with roasted cherry tomatoes makes a festive presentation.

¾ cup fresh fine bread crumbs

⅓ cup whole milk

¾ teaspoon fennel seeds

8 ounces ground pork

2 large cloves garlic, minced

¼ teaspoon paprika

1 teaspoon sea or kosher salt

½ teaspoon freshly ground black pepper

12 cleaned small whole squid bodies, about 6 inches long, plus their tentacles (about 1 pound total)

3 tablespoons extra-virgin olive oil

Olive oil for the grill rack

1 tablespoon chopped fresh flat-leaf parsley

Lemon wedges for serving

1 To make the stuffing, in a large bowl, soak the bread crumbs in the milk.

2 In a dry nonstick frying pan over medium heat, toast the fennel seeds, shaking the pan often, until fragrant, about 3 minutes. Pour onto a cutting board. Chop the fennel seeds and add to the moistened bread crumbs along with the pork, garlic, paprika, ½ teaspoon of the salt, and ¼ teaspoon of the pepper. Mix gently with your hands until well blended.

3 Using a small spoon or your fingers, loosely fill the squid bodies with the stuffing. Secure the top of each squid closed with a toothpick. Rub the stuffed bodies and the tentacles with the extra-virgin olive oil and season with the remaining ½ teaspoon salt.

4 Prepare a medium fire in a wood or charcoal grill or preheat a gas grill to medium.

5 When the fire is ready, rub the grill rack with olive oil. Place the stuffed squid on the rack directly over the fire and grill, turning often, until golden in spots and an instant-read thermometer inserted through the top into the center of the stuffing registers 150°F, about 15 minutes. Transfer the stuffed squid to a platter. Place the tentacles in a grilling basket directly over the fire and grill, turning the basket two or three times, until opaque, about 3 minutes.

6 Scatter the tentacles over the squid, then sprinkle the parsley and the remaining ¼ teaspoon pepper over all. Add a handful of lemon wedges to the platter and serve.

Makes 12 stuffed squid; serves 4

Pork Country Sausage

This recipe has passed the breakfast sausage taste test of my husband, an Englishman who is discerning about his breakfasts. It's not complicated, which makes it a good starting point for sausage making. Georgeanne and I both make several types of sausage and freeze them as part of our kitchen pantry. The sausage can be used on its own, to flavor sauces, or for crumbling onto pizzas. Stuffing sausage into casings is an extra step, one that is always easier to do with two people.

6 pounds pork belly trimmings or boneless pork butt, cut into 1-inch cubes

3 tablespoons sea or kosher salt

1 tablespoon freshly ground black pepper

¼ cup mixed minced fresh flat-leaf parsley, thyme, rosemary, and sage in equal parts

3½ tablespoons chopped garlic (about 4 cloves)

1½ cups dry red wine such as Pinot Noir, Zinfandel, or Merlot

2 pounds large hog casings (optional)

1 Chill the meat, two large bowls, and all of the metal parts of the meat grinder and of the sausage stuffer, if using.

2 In one of the chilled bowls, combine the meat, salt, and pepper and mix well. Put the large-holed plate in the meat grinder and grind the seasoned meat into the second chilled bowl. Add the herbs, garlic, and wine to the meat and mix well. Fit the meat grinder with the medium-holed plate and grind the mixture again.

3 Shape a nugget of the meat mixture into a small patty. In a small frying pan over medium heat, fry the patty, turning once, until cooked through, a few minutes on each side. Taste and then adjust the seasoning in the meat mixture as needed. If you will not be stuffing the meat mixture into casings, shape it into patties or into practical-size bulk amounts and place in ziplock plastic bags. Refrigerate what will be used promptly and freeze the balance for up to 6 months.

4 To stuff the meat mixture into casings, remove the plate and knife from the grinder and attach the large stuffing tube. The casings come packed in salt, so rinse them thoroughly inside and out before you begin. Large hog casings will yield sausages about 1 inch in diameter. Fit a roughly 5-foot length of casing onto the tube, leaving a 4- to 5-inch tail. With a pestle, push the meat mixture through the tube into the casing. As you work, hold the casing at the tube and guide the meat down into the casing so that it is full but not tight and no air pockets form. When the mixture fills the far end, squeeze the air out of the end and tie a knot in the casing, then continue to fill the casing. Every 4 to 5 inches, spin the filled casing to twist it into links, alternating the direction of the spin with each link. If you are working by yourself, you can twist the filled casing into links after the entire casing is stuffed. If bubbles develop, prick them with a sausage pricker or a pin. Just before the end of the casing is reached, remove it from the tube and tie it off tightly against the filling. Continue with other lengths of casing until all of the meat mixture is used. Refrigerate the sausages that will be used promptly and freeze the remainder for up to 6 months. Any leftover casings can be drained well, packed in salt, and stored in the refrigerator for up to 1 year.

Makes 6 pounds sausage, or 28 to 36 sausage links each 4 to 5 inches long

Chile Relleno Casserole with Red Sauce

Ann and I are both fond of chiles rellenos and we often order them when lunchtime finds us at a Mexican restaurant. Since making them at home can be labor-intensive, I created this simple dish that has all of the taste and texture of the classic chile relleno, but not the batter dipping and frying. I use either long, bright green Anaheim chiles, which are readily available at the market by late summer, or dark green poblanos, which start appearing in early fall. Either of the tomato sauces in the book will work with this dish, or use your own favorite homemade or purchased light tomato sauce.

8 Anaheim or poblano chiles

4 to 6 ounces Monterey Jack or other mild cheese

8 eggs, separated

¼ cup all-purpose flour

½ teaspoon fine sea salt

1 to 1½ cups tomato sauce, homemade (page 136 or 213) or purchased

1. Preheat the broiler.

2. Place the chiles on a baking sheet, slide under the broiler about 4 inches from the heat source, and broil, turning as needed to char evenly, until lightly charred and blistered on all sides, about 5 minutes. Transfer the chiles to a plastic bag to sweat for 15 minutes. Remove the chiles from the bag and peel away the skin. Make a lengthwise slit on one side of each chile and remove and discard the seeds, leaving the stem intact.

3. Cut the cheese into slices about 4 inches long and a generous ¼ inch thick. Slip a slice into each chile through the slit. Place in the refrigerator.

4. Preheat the oven to 375°F.

5. To make the batter, in a large bowl, using an electric mixer, beat the egg whites on medium speed until foamy. Increase the speed to medium-high and beat until stiff peaks form. Sprinkle in the flour and continue to beat until all of the flour has been incorporated and

6. Spread a thin layer of the tomato sauce (about ¼ cup) in the bottom of a 9-inch square baking dish. Lay the stuffed chiles, slit side up, on the sauce. Spread the batter evenly over the chiles. Bake until puffed and golden, about 25 minutes.

7. To serve, heat the remaining tomato sauce. Using a spatula, transfer 2 stuffed chiles to each plate. Pass the warm tomato sauce at the table.

Serves 4

Creamy Grits with Collard Greens and Wild Mushrooms

Fall is the time the market starts to turn to greens—collards, kale, mustard, chard—and any one of them can be used to make this simple, hearty recipe. I had never prepared collards because I thought they had to cook a long, long time, and because I'd only eaten them once or twice and didn't have much of a taste memory. Then Ann told me that you could cook them in just 15 or 20 minutes, as long as the stems were removed and the leaves finely chopped or julienned. I did as she told me and became a convert, and now collards are one of my staples. We are fortunate to have a mushroom vendor, Solano Mushroom Farm, year-round at the Davis Farmers Market, but in fall, look especially for their wild-gathered chanterelles and porcini.

4 cups water

1 cup stone-ground grits (not instant)

Sea salt or kosher salt and freshly ground black pepper

8 tablespoons (1 cube) unsalted butter

1 bunch collards (about 12 leaves), stems removed and leaves julienned

2 to 3 tablespoons water

2 tablespoons minced yellow onion

4 cups mixed wild mushrooms (8 to 12 ounces), any kind, trimmed and left whole if small, quartered or halved if large

1 In a saucepan over medium-high heat, bring the water to a boil. Add the grits slowly, stirring to prevent clumping. Reduce the heat to low. Cook uncovered, stirring from time to time, until most of the water has been absorbed, 20 to 25 minutes. Season with salt and pepper.

2 While the grits are cooking, in a frying pan or sauté pan over medium heat, melt 4 tablespoons of the butter. When it foams, add the greens, stir quickly, and then add a few tablespoons of water. Cover with a tight-fitting lid, reduce the heat to low, and simmer until the greens are soft and tender to the bite and most of the water has evaporated, about 15 minutes.

3 In a frying pan or sauté pan over medium heat, melt the remaining 4 tablespoons butter. When it foams, add the onion and cook, stirring, until translucent, 2 to 3 minutes. Add the mushrooms, stir well, reduce the heat to low, and continue to cook until the mushrooms are tender and most of the juices they released have been absorbed, about 5 minutes. Season with salt and pepper.

4 To serve, divide the grits among warmed individual soup bowls. Spoon the mushrooms onto the center of the grits and then top with the greens. Serve right away.

Serves 4

Roasted Lamb Shanks with Dried Fruits

Lamb shanks are one of the most succulent cuts when slowly braised. Here we have added a mix of some of the many different kinds of dried fruits available at the market, which gives the final dish a hint of the sweetness found in classic Moroccan dishes that combine the same ingredients. Serve the shanks with couscous or rice.

1 cup mixed dried fruits such as Pluots, apricots, and peaches or nectarines

4 small lamb shanks (about 1½ pounds each), or 2 large lamb shanks (about 3 pounds each)

Sea salt and freshly ground black pepper

¼ cup extra-virgin olive oil

½ yellow onion, finely chopped

2 cloves garlic, minced

¼ cup dry white wine

2 to 3 cups chicken stock, homemade (page 48) or purchased

4 fresh thyme sprigs

1 bay leaf

1 teaspoon minced fresh rosemary

¼ cup golden raisins

1 Preheat the oven to 325°F.

2 Cut any large dried fruits in half; leave smaller ones, such as apricots, whole. Set aside.

3 Rub the lamb shanks all over with salt and pepper to season them well. In a Dutch oven over medium-high heat, warm the olive oil. When it is hot, add the shanks and cook, turning as needed, until browned well on all sides, 5 to 7 minutes. Transfer to a platter.

4 Pour off all but 2 tablespoons of the fat from the pan and return the pan to medium-high heat. Add the onion and sauté until translucent, about 2 minutes. Add the garlic and stir briefly. Increase the heat to high, pour in the wine, and scrape the pan bottom to dislodge any clinging browned bits. Add 2 cups of the stock, the thyme, the bay leaf, and the rosemary, then return the shanks to the pan and bring to a simmer.

5 Remove from the heat, cover, and place in the oven. Cook, turning several times, until the meat is easily cut through with a fork, about 1½ hours. If the liquid appears to have diminished, add more of the stock as needed to keep the shanks moist. Add half of the dried fruits, cover, and continue to cook for another 10 minutes.

6 Remove the pan from the oven and place on the stove top over medium heat. Stir in the remaining dried fruits and the raisins, bring to a simmer, and simmer until the fruits are heated through.

7 If you have used small shanks, transfer them to warmed individual plates. If you have used large shanks, remove the meat from the bones and divide the meat among warmed individual plates. Spoon the fruits and cooking juices over the shanks and serve right away.

Serves 4

Musquée de Provence with New Crop Walnuts

The Musquée de Provence pumpkin, sometimes called the Fairy Tale pumpkin, is deeply lobed and its color ranges from buff to almost burnished copper. Its dark orange flesh is dense, meaty, and full of flavor. The Davis market vendors often sell it in wedges, just like it is sold in France, so it is easy to buy just enough for a meal rather than an entire pumpkin, which can weigh up to twenty pounds. The Musquée de Provence and other pumpkins appear in the market at about the same time as the new crop of walnuts, which are moist and sweet with fresh oil.

8 (1-inch-thick) slices Musquée de Provence pumpkin

¼ cup extra-virgin olive oil

2 teaspoons ground cumin

Sea salt and freshly ground black pepper

1 cup coarsely chopped walnuts

2 tablespoons walnut oil

1. Preheat the oven to 350°F.
2. Place the pumpkin slices in a bowl or baking dish and toss with the olive oil, coating them evenly on both sides. Arrange the slices in a single layer on two baking sheets and sprinkle with the cumin, salt, and pepper.
3. Roast for 15 minutes, then sprinkle with the walnuts. Continue to roast until tender when pierced with a fork, about 15 minutes more.
4. Transfer to a large warmed platter or individual plates and drizzle each slice with a little walnut oil. Serve hot.

Serves 8

RICH COLLINS, OWNER OF CALIFORNIA VEGETABLE SPECIALTIES, AT HIS BELGIAN ENDIVE PRODUCTION FACILITY IN RIO VISTA, CALIFORNIA.

Braised Belgian Endive

We are fortunate to have locally grown Belgian endives at the market. California Vegetable Specialties, located in Rio Vista, about fifty miles south of Davis, is the only commercial grower of Belgian endive in the United States, and Rich Collins, the innovative owner, has been our friend for many years. The endives are field grown, then the roots are dug, trimmed, and put in cold storage. The roots are brought out of storage and hydroponically grown in the dark to force the growth of the tight head, or chicon, that we know as Belgian endive. It is a versatile vegetable that can be eaten raw in salads, braised, baked, made into gratins, grilled, or roasted.

8 heads Belgian endive

2 tablespoons unsalted butter

1 teaspoon sea or kosher salt

½ cup chicken stock or vegetable stock, homemade (page 48) or purchased

1. Cut the endives in half lengthwise, then remove the hard cone at the base. In a sauté pan or frying pan over medium-high heat, melt the butter. When it foams, add the endive halves, cut side down, and sauté until lightly golden, 5 to 6 minutes. Turn the halves over and sauté on the second side until golden, 4 to 5 minutes. Reduce the heat to low, sprinkle with the salt, and add the stock. Cover and continue to cook until easily pierced with the tines of a fork, about 20 minutes.

2. Transfer to a warmed platter and serve hot.

Serves 4

Persimmon Flan

This is one of those recipes that is just too good not to resurrect. I first created it for my book *Potager*, which is now out of print. Ann loves the recipes in *Potager* and found a used copy online. Made with the jellylike pulp of the burnt orange–colored Hachiya persimmon, the final flan has one layer of dense persimmon that sinks into the caramelized sugar and one layer of sweet custard.

1 cup sugar	1 cup whole milk
2 or 3 very ripe, soft Hachiya persimmons, peeled, seeded, and cut into 1½-inch pieces	6 eggs
	½ teaspoon fine sea or kosher salt
2 cups heavy cream	1 teaspoon vanilla extract

1. Spread ½ cup of the sugar in an 8-inch metal pie pan and place it over medium heat. Holding the edge of the pan with a hot pad, tilt the pan from side to side as the sugar melts and caramelizes so that the bottom as well as the sides is coated with the syrup. When all of the sugar has melted into a golden to dark brown liquid, remove the pan from the stove. Set aside.

2. In a saucepan over medium-high heat, cook the persimmon pieces, stirring often to prevent sticking or burning, until they release some of their moisture and thicken a bit, about 5 minutes. Remove from the heat and let cool slightly.

3. Transfer the persimmons to a blender and purée until smooth. Pass the purée though a chinois or a fine-mesh sieve. You should have about ¾ cup purée.

4. Preheat the oven to 325°F. Fill a teakettle with water and bring the water to a boil.

5. In a saucepan over medium heat, combine the cream and milk and heat until small bubbles form around the edges of the pan. Remove from the heat. In a large bowl, whisk the eggs just until blended, then add the remaining ½ cup sugar, the salt, and the vanilla and whisk until thoroughly combined. Slowly pour the hot milk-cream mixture into the eggs while whisking or stirring continuously. Stir in the puréed fruit.

6 Place the caramel-lined pie pan in a shallow roasting pan just large enough to hold it. Pour the custard mixture into the pie pan, filling it to the rim. Pour the boiling water into the roasting pan to reach halfway up the sides of the pie pan.

7 Bake the flan until a knife inserted into the middle comes out clean, 35 to 45 minutes.

8 Remove the roasting pan from the oven and remove the flan. Let cool to room temperature. At this point, the flan can be refrigerated for up to several hours.

9 To unmold the flan, slide a knife blade or thin metal spatula around the inside edge of the pan to loosen the flan sides. Invert a serving plate on top of the pan and, holding the pan and the plate firmly together, flip them. Lift off the flan pan. To serve, cut into wedges.

Serves 8 to 10

Sautéed Quinces, Apples, and Pears with Whipped Cream

Quince, like the apple and so many other fruits, is a member of the rose family. It has a texture that is a little coarser than that of an apple and a sweet aroma when fully ripe, and both Georgeanne and I appreciate it for its versatility and its history. Once commonly seen growing at the end of a country lane or bordering a homestead, quinces are now difficult to find, a forgotten fruit. Fortunately, Dianne Madison of Yolo Bulb and Yolo Press brings part of her crop to the market.

1½ cups heavy cream

2 tablespoons sugar

½ teaspoon vanilla extract

4 tablespoons unsalted butter

3 quinces, peeled, halved, cored, and sliced ½ inch thick

2 apples, halved, cored, and sliced ½ inch thick

2 pears, halved, cored, and sliced ½ inch thick

1 In a bowl, using an electric mixer, beat the cream on medium-high speed until soft peaks form, 3 to 4 minutes. Add the sugar and vanilla and continue to beat on medium-high speed until stiff peaks form, about 4 minutes longer. Cover and refrigerate until serving.

2 In a large frying pan over medium heat, melt the butter. When it foams, add the fruit slices and sauté until golden on the first side, about 5 minutes. Turn the slices and sauté on the second side until golden and just tender, about 5 minutes longer.

3 Divide the slices among individual plates, top with the whipped cream, and serve. Or, to serve family style, transfer the slices to a platter and pass the whipped cream at the table.

Serves 6 to 8

Old-Fashioned Butter Cookies with Pistachios

In the last few decades, pistachios have become a big crop in California. The state grows not only almost all of the pistachios harvested in the United States but also almost one-fourth of the world crop, making it second in production only to Iran. We are fortunate to have our own pistachio grower, Fiddyment Farms, that faithfully brings nuts to the market.

2 cups all-purpose flour

¼ teaspoon sea or kosher salt

1 cup (2 cubes) unsalted butter, at room temperature

1 cup sugar

1 teaspoon almond or vanilla extract

1 teaspoon minced lemon zest

2 teaspoons honey

1 egg

1 cup chopped pistachio nuts, plus about ⅓ cup whole nuts

1 Preheat the oven to 375°F. Line a baking sheet with parchment paper.

2 In a bowl, stir together the flour and salt and reserve. In a stand mixer fitted with the paddle attachment, or in a bowl with an electric mixer, cream together the butter and sugar on medium speed until light and fluffy, 2 to 3 minutes. Add the almond extract, lemon zest, and honey and beat until combined, then add the egg and beat until combined. On low speed, add the flour mixture and mix just until thoroughly incorporated, about 1 minute. Add the chopped pistachios and stir with a wooden spoon until evenly distributed throughout the dough.

3 Scoop up nuggets of the dough, roll between your palms into 1-inch balls, and place on the prepared baking sheet, spacing them about 1½ inches apart. When all of the dough has been shaped, using a wooden spoon, flatten each ball to about ½ inch thick. Place a whole pistachio in the center of each cookie.

4 Bake the cookies until the edges are lightly browned, 10 to 12 minutes. Transfer to a rack and let cool completely. The cookies will keep in an airtight container at room temperature for up to 1 week or in the freezer for 2 months.

Makes about 36 cookies

CHUTNEY MAKING

Chutneys are essentially fruit pickles that often include vegetables and spices as well. They can be sweet or hot and they vary from country to country. For example, in India and Pakistan, the chutneys are often dark and dense and nearly every meal includes at least two or three types. Chutneys are also an essential part of a *rijsttafel*, literally "rice table," a multicourse feast of small dishes that originated with Dutch colonialists in Indonesia. In English and American cooking, chutneys are often similar to classic pickled vegetables, with the fruit cooked just enough to tenderize it. Of course, as with all traditional foods, lines are crossed and many variations are not only possible but acceptable.

In fall, the market is filled with both late-summer and early fall fruits and vegetables, making it a perfect time for chutney making. For the best flavor, chutneys should age for a least a month before they are served, so putting up some now ensures they'll be ready for your holiday table. They can be served as a side to roast meats, soups, or stews, to accompany cheeses, as a sandwich spread, or as part of a condiment tray or charcuterie.

FALL FRUIT CHUTNEY

You will need two pint canning jars with lids and rings, a canning kettle with a rack and cover (or a large, wide pot with a wire rack and cover) for the water bath, a large, heavy nonreactive pot for cooking the chutney, canning tongs, and a ladle.

2 pounds stone fruits such as plums, nectarines, or Pluots, pitted and coarsely chopped

1 pound apples, cored and coarsely chopped

8 ounces yellow onions, coarsely chopped

4 cloves garlic, minced

1/3 cup firmly packed light brown sugar

2-inch piece fresh ginger, peeled and minced (about 2 tablespoons)

1 teaspoon sea or kosher salt

1 cinnamon stick, about 2 inches long

2 teaspoons minced lemon zest

1 cup cider vinegar

1/2 green jalapeño or other hot chile, seeded and finely chopped

1 tablespoon black peppercorns

In the large, heavy nonreactive pot, combine all of the ingredients and bring to a boil over medium heat. Reduce the heat to low and cook, stirring occasionally to prevent scorching, until all of the ingredients are soft and blended, about 3 hours. Once the mixture starts to thicken, stir more frequently to prevent burning.

Meanwhile, set up the water bath. Fill the canning kettle with water (the water must be deep enough to cover the jars by 1 to 2 inches) and bring to a boil over high heat. If you don't have a canning kettle, use a large, wide pot and put a wire rack in the bottom of the pot before you fill it with water. Once the water boils, you can turn off the heat and then return it to a boil just before you put the jars in the kettle.

Wash the canning jars in hot, soapy water and rinse well. Place the jars in a saucepan, add water to cover generously, and bring to a boil over medium-high heat. Boil for 15 minutes, then turn off the heat and leave the jars in the hot water until you are ready to fill them. Fill another saucepan half full with water and bring to a boil over medium-high heat. Add the canning lids and rings and boil for 5 minutes. Turn off the heat and leave the lids and rings in the hot water until needed.

Just before the chutney is ready, using tongs, transfer the jars to a work surface. Return the water in the canning kettle to a boil. Ladle the hot chutney into the hot, sterilized jars, filling them to within ½ inch of the rim. With a clean, damp cloth, wipe the rim of each jar. Place a lid on the rim and then screw on a ring, being careful not to screw it on too tightly. Using canning tongs, put the filled jars into the rack of the canner and lower the rack into the boiling water. If you are using a large, wide pot, use the canning tongs to lower the jars onto the rack in the bottom of the pot, making sure the jars do not touch. Return the water to a rolling boil, reduce the heat slightly, cover, and boil for 10 minutes.

Cover a work surface with a folded towel. Using the canning tongs, transfer the jars to the towel, spacing them a few inches apart. As the jars begin to cool, you may hear popping sounds, which is the sound of the lids sealing. The lids should be indented. When the jars are completely cool, after at least 12 hours, check the seal on each jar by pressing on the center of the lid. If it remains indented, the seal is good. If it does not, refrigerate the jar and use the chutney within 1 month.

Label the jars with the contents and date and store in a cool, dry place for up to 1 year.

Makes 2 pints

Pomegranate Jelly

Juicing pomegranates is a messy business, but Georgeanne and I both think the end result is worth the stains. When it is jelly-making time, I head outside in old clothes with my manual juice extractor, the kind with a spring-loaded lever and press, and plenty of newspapers. As with all jellies, to keep the correct ratio for jelling, it is better to make individual batches rather than double or triple a recipe. I now have a copper confiture pot from France, a prized possession I found in an old cook shop in Paris, in which I make all my jellies and jams.

You will need three pint or six half-pint canning jars with lids and rings, a canning kettle with a rack and cover (or a large, wide pot with a wire rack and cover) for the water bath, a heavy, nonreactive saucepan for cooking the jelly, canning tongs, and a ladle.

20 to 25 pomegranates	¼ cup fresh lemon juice
1 package (1¾ ounces) powdered pectin	5 cups sugar

1 To set up the water bath, fill the canning kettle with water (the water must be deep enough to cover the jars by 1 to 2 inches) and bring to a boil over high heat. If you don't have a canning kettle, use a large, wide pot and put a wire rack in the bottom of the pot before you fill it with water. Once the water boils, you can turn off the heat and then return it to a boil just before you put the jars in the kettle.

2 Wash the canning jars in hot, soapy water and rinse well. Place the jars in a saucepan, add water to cover generously, and bring to a boil over medium-high heat. Boil for 15 minutes, then turn off the heat and leave the jars in the hot water until you are ready to fill them. Fill another saucepan half full with water and bring to a boil over medium-high heat. Add the canning lids and rings and boil for 5 minutes. Turn off the heat and leave the lids and rings in the hot water until needed.

3 Cut the pomegranates in half. Put each half in a manual juice extractor (a heavy-duty orange juicer will work) and squeeze out the juice. When finished, strain the juice through a chinois or a fine-mesh sieve lined with cheesecloth into a large measuring cup. Measure exactly 3½ cups.

4 Pour the strained juice into the heavy, nonreactive saucepan, add the pectin and lemon juice, and stir for several minutes to dissolve the pectin thoroughly. Place the pan over medium heat and bring the mixture to a boil, stirring constantly. Stir in the sugar and continue to stir until the mixture is at a rolling boil, then boil for 1 minute. Remove from the heat and skim off any foam that has formed on top.

5 Just before the jelly mixture is ready, using tongs, transfer the jars to a work surface. Return the water in the canning kettle to a boil. Ladle the hot mixture into the hot, sterilized jars, filling them to within 1/2 inch of the rim. With a clean, damp cloth, wipe the rim of each jar. Place a lid on the rim and then screw on a ring, being careful not to screw it on too tightly. Using canning tongs, put the filled jars into the rack of the canner and lower the rack into the boiling water. If you are using a large, wide pot, use the canning tongs to lower the jars onto the rack in the bottom of the pot, making sure the jars do not touch. Return the water to a rolling boil, reduce the heat slightly, cover, and boil for 5 minutes.

6 Cover a work surface with a folded towel. Using the canning tongs, transfer the jars to the towel, spacing them a few inches apart. As the jars begin to cool, you may hear popping sounds, which is the sound of the lids sealing. The lids should be indented. When the jars are completely cool, after at least 12 hours, check the seal on each jar by pressing on the center of the lid. If it remains indented, the seal is good. If it does not, refrigerate the jar and use the jelly within 1 month.

7 Label the jars with the contents and date and store in a cool, dry place for up to 1 year.

Makes 3 pints or 6 half-pints

Winter
the Dormant Season

In winter's short, cold days, fruit trees are dormant and the traditional fruits and vegetables of the season are either those that have already been harvested and stored or those that thrive in the field or garden relatively undamaged by frost. These are complemented by citrus fruits of all kinds. Winter is also Dungeness crab season, and when the crustaceans make their first appearance in November, the fish stall is well stocked. Local olives are pressed in the winter months as well, and market vendors offer the freshly pressed oil, *olio nuovo* in Italian, full of the immediate flavor and scent of olives and olive leaves, that is available only in winter.

The market stalls are now filled with oranges, lemons, grapefruits, and mandarins, tempting the cook to combine them with winter's slightly bitter greens, such as escarole and radicchio, or crunchy licorice-flavored fennel. Leeks, winter carrots and beets, storage potatoes and onions, cabbages, cauliflower, Brussels sprouts, and broccoli assure the cook of plenty of vegetables for gratins and braises, roasting and stir-frying.

Pumpkins and winter squashes, which made a brief appearance in fall in time for Halloween, are now plentiful and will be throughout the season. Summer's basil has been blackened by frost, and winter's herbs are the hardy, woody ones, like rosemary, oregano, thyme, and winter savory.

Crab Salad on Belgian Endive Leaves with Avocado

Belgian endive leaves are perfect little boats to carry the taste of an appetizer, which can be as simple as a nubbin of goat cheese and a bit of smoked salmon finished with a caper or as fancy as this crab salad. Since the endives are available year-round, using them for a winter appetizer is easy. Williamson Produce of San Diego brings ripe avocados to the market year-round as well.

6 heads Belgian endive

2 cups cooked crabmeat (from about 1 medium crab, see page 211), picked over for shells

2 tablespoons mayonnaise

½ teaspoon fresh lemon juice

½ Granny Smith apple, peeled, cored, and minced

1 tablespoon minced fresh tarragon

1 tablespoon minced fresh chives

2 teaspoons extra-virgin olive oil

Sea or kosher salt

1 avocado, halved, pitted, peeled, and each half cut into 12 thin slices

1 Cut about ½ inch off the base of each endive head and remove the larger outer leaves, reserving the smaller ones for another use. You should have 24 leaves. Tear the crabmeat into pieces and place in a bowl. Add the mayonnaise, lemon juice, apple, tarragon, chives, and olive oil and mix gently. Season with salt.

2 Place a generous teaspoon of the crab mixture on the base of each Belgian endive leaf and garnish with an avocado slice. Arrange on a platter and serve.

Makes 24; serves 6 to 8

Devils on Horseback

Fresh dates come to market from California's Coachella Valley. One winter, Ann and I took a trip to visit Leja Farms, which sells their dates at the Davis Farmers Market, and wandered among the trees, heavy with long bunches of fruit. We felt like we were characters in a tale from the Arabian Nights. We sampled the Deglet Noors, Medjools, and Barhis. All were sweet and dense and their flavors distinct, with the small, honeyed yellow-gold Barhis the sweetest. For this retro appetizer, which has waxed and waned in popularity since at least the 1970s, any dates can be used. This dish is a companion piece to angels on horseback, in which oysters or scallops replace the dates.

16 dates

16 slivers Parmesan cheese

6 slices bacon, each cut into thirds

1. Preheat the oven to 450°F.

2. Cut a lengthwise slit in each date, being careful not to cut all the way through, and remove the pit. Tuck a sliver of cheese into each date, then wrap the date with a piece of the bacon and fasten it with a toothpick. Place the dates on a rimmed baking sheet.

3. Bake the dates until the bacon is lightly crisped, about 5 minutes. Transfer to paper towels to drain briefly, then arrange on a platter and serve hot or warm.

Makes 16; serves 6 to 8

Shiitake Mushroom Soup Shots

This soup is all about the earthy flavor of shiitake mushrooms, but it relies heavily on the stock to bring out their flavor. I am using Georgeanne's leek and mushroom stock, one of her favorite all-purpose vegetable stocks. The soup, though rich with flavor, is surprisingly light and refreshing and will meet the needs of all of your guests, if, like me, your family table is a mix of vegans, vegetarians, and carnivores.

Stock

- ¼ pound mixed mushrooms, any kind, coarsely chopped
- Stems from shiitake mushrooms for soup (below), coarsely chopped
- 2 carrots, cut into 2-inch lengths
- 1 large leek, cut into 2-inch lengths
- 1 yellow onion, quartered
- 2 whole cloves
- 3 cups water
- ½ teaspoon sea or kosher salt

Soup

- 3 tablespoons coconut oil
- ½ cup peeled and coarsely chopped carrot
- 1 tablespoon peeled and minced fresh ginger
- ½ pound shiitake mushrooms, stems removed and reserved for stock and caps chopped (about 3 cups)
- 1 tablespoon canola oil
- 4 to 6 fresh chives, minced

1 To make the stock, in a saucepan, combine all of the ingredients and bring to a boil over medium-high heat. Cover, reduce the heat to low, and simmer until the vegetables have imparted their flavor to the stock, 45 minutes to 1 hour. Remove from the heat and strain through a chinois or a colander lined with cheesecloth. Measure 2¼ cups and set aside.

2 To make the soup, in a large sauté pan over medium-high heat, warm the coconut oil. When it is hot, add the carrots and ginger and sauté until the carrots soften, about

3 minutes. Set aside about ¼ cup of the chopped mushrooms for garnish, then add the remaining mushrooms to the carrot mixture and sauté until lightly browned, about 1 minute. Reduce the heat to low, cover, and continue cooking for 5 minutes. Remove from the heat and let cool slightly.

3 In a food processor, combine the mushroom-carrot mixture and the 2¼ cups stock and process until smooth, 1 to 2 minutes. Transfer the soup to a saucepan and keep warm.

4 Finely chop the reserved ¼ cup chopped mushrooms. In a small sauté pan over medium heat, warm the canola oil. Add the finely chopped mushrooms and sauté, stirring frequently, until golden brown, about 2 minutes. Remove from the heat.

5 Reheat the soup until hot, then divide evenly among shot glasses (¼-cup capacity). Garnish each serving with a sprinkle of chives and 2 or 3 pieces of sautéed mushroom. Serve at once.

Serves 8 to 10

HOMEMADE PANCETTA

Traditionally, farm families have prepared sausage, ham, bacon, and other pork products in the winter, when it is cold out and the meat won't spoil. Many families make a two-day party of it to get all parts of the pig processed and preserved for the coming year. John Bledsoe and his son, who sell pork, pork belly, and all parts pork, including fatback, trotters, heads, and jowls, as well as lamb, at the market, provided the pork belly, which can be purchased by special order. When hogs are butchered, the whole bellies are split in half lengthwise; you are using just half for this recipe, though the cut is often labeled "whole pork belly" in meat markets. Pancetta creates extra layers of flavor in any dish to which it is added.

SPICE MIXTURE

3 star anise pods

3 cinnamon sticks, about 2 inches long, broken

3 tablespoons cumin seeds

3 teaspoons whole cloves

3 teaspoons ground coriander

1 cup sea or kosher salt

⅔ cup sugar

---

1 pork belly with skin intact, about 10 pounds

7 cloves garlic, finely chopped

½ cup sea or kosher salt

½ cup firmly packed light brown sugar

4 bay leaves, crushed

3 tablespoons chopped fresh rosemary

2 tablespoons freshly coarse-ground black pepper, plus 2 to 4 tablespoons freshly cracked

1 tablespoon chopped fresh sage

1 tablespoon fennel and/or coriander seeds, crushed

1 tablespoon juniper berries, crushed

1 tablespoon granulated sugar

¼ cup spice mixture

To make the spice mixture, in a spice grinder, combine the star anise, cinnamon, cumin, and cloves and grind finely. Transfer to a bowl, add the coriander, salt, and sugar, and stir well. Measure out ¼ cup and set aside to use for the pancetta. Store the remainder in an airtight container in the refrigerator for up to 6 months to use for your next batch of pancetta.

Lay the pork belly flat, with the skin and fat side up and the meat side down. Using the tip of a sharp knife, cut the skin off of the slab, pulling it back with your free hand as you cut. Trim the edges to even the belly into a rectangle. Cut it in half crosswise; even out each slab by trimming the edges. You should have two 8-by-10-by-1-inch slabs of fat and meat.

In a bowl, stir together the garlic, salt, brown sugar, bay leaves, rosemary, 2 tablespoons coarse-ground pepper, sage, fennel and/or coriander, juniper berries, granulated sugar, and the spice mixture, mixing well. Rub the belly slabs on both sides with the seasoning mix, covering them completely and evenly. Put each slab in a ziplock plastic bag and seal each bag, forcing out the air. Place the bags flat in the refrigerator and top each bag with a weight. I use a couple of cookbooks for weights.

Turn the slabs every day for 7 days. The slabs will become very wet and the fat will become hard.

Remove the slabs from the bags, rinse off the cure, and pat the slabs dry. Place each slab on a tray with the fat side down and the meat side up. (You want the fat to be on the outside as you roll the slab.) Rub the meat side of each slab with the cracked peppercorns, using the larger amount if you like your pancetta peppery.

Starting at the end closest to you, roll up a slab tightly, making sure to eliminate any air pockets. Tie the roll tightly with cotton string, looping the string twice around the length of the roll and spacing the loops ¼ inch apart to create a cross on top. Then create netting with butchers' knots or macramé—or just tie any knot you know how to tie—to secure the pancetta along its length, spacing the knots at ½- to 1-inch intervals. The tighter the netting and more evenly spaced the knots, the better the roll will dry. Repeat with the second slab.

Loop a 3-foot length of string through each pancetta at the cross on one end, then tie the string securely over a shelf in the refrigerator. Make sure there is enough space around each roll for the air to circulate freely. This may require removing a shelf.

Leave the rolls hanging until the meat is firm and dry, 2 to 3 weeks.

When the pancetta is ready, reserve about one-third in the refrigerator to use. It will keep for up to 6 weeks. Put the other two-thirds in ziplock plastic bags and seal, forcing out the air. Freeze for up to 6 months.

Makes two 5-pound rolls

Fried Oyster Sliders with Homemade Tartar Sauce

In West Marin County, Drake's Bay and Tomales Bay specifically, you'll find some of the finest Pacific oysters anywhere. Ann and I can attest to that because she goes there for barbecue cookouts, buying oysters by the bag, and I usually take mine home and eat them raw. We can also find them in season at the market, both by the jar and in the shell. For fried oysters, I buy the jarred ones because it is easier than shucking, a chore at which I am not very adept. Small buns for this dish can be ordered from one of the market bakeries.

Tartar Sauce	Oysters
1 cup mayonnaise	2 eggs, beaten
1 teaspoon Dijon mustard	1 cup all-purpose flour
3 tablespoons finely chopped sweet pickle	Canola or other light vegetable oil for frying
2 tablespoons minced green onion, about two-thirds white and one-third green	12 shucked fresh oysters
1 teaspoon sweet pickle juice	12 slider buns, 2½ to 3 inches in diameter
½ teaspoon fresh lemon juice	

1 To make the tartar sauce, in a bowl, combine all of the ingredients and mix well.

2 To prepare the oysters, pour the beaten eggs onto a shallow plate. Spread the flour on a second shallow plate. Pour the oil to a depth of about 1 inch in a large, deep sauté pan or frying pan and heat over medium-high heat. When the oil is hot, dredge an oyster first in the eggs, allowing the excess to drip off, then in the flour, shaking off the excess, and slide the oyster into the hot oil. Repeat with another 5 oysters; they should not be crowded in the pan. Cook until golden on the bottom, about 1 minute. Turn and cook the other side until golden, about 1 minute longer. Using a slotted spoon or spatula, transfer the oysters to a plate or platter covered with paper towels. Keep warm while you cook the remaining oysters in the same way.

3 To serve, spread both cut sides of each bun with the tartar sauce. Place a fried oyster on the bottom half of each bun and close with the top half. Serve hot.

Makes 12 sliders; serves 6

Fried Smelt with Rouille Dipping Sauce

We can often find Pacific Ocean smelt at the market. I buy them whenever I see them, just like the sardines, and I taught Ann how to cook them. In my house, crispy fried smelt, known affectionately as fish fries, are eaten whole—heads, tails, and all—with no cleaning needed before cooking and just a dusting of flour. They can be eaten out of hand, like French fries, with a squeeze of lemon or a flavored mayonnaise such as rouille or aioli, the same way they are served at restaurants from San Francisco to Nice.

1½ pounds smelt

1 cup all-purpose flour

Canola oil or other light vegetable oil for frying

2 teaspoons sea or kosher salt

1 teaspoon freshly ground black pepper

1 cup rouille (page 99)

4 lemons, quartered

1 Pat the fish dry. Spread the flour on a shallow plate. Pour the oil to a depth of about 1 inch into a deep sauté pan or frying pan and heat over medium-high heat. When the oil is hot, dredge a handful or two of the smelt in the flour, shaking off the excess, and slide them into the hot oil, being careful not to crowd the pan. Cook until golden on the bottom, about 1 minute. Turn and cook the other side until golden, about 1 minute longer. Using a slotted spoon or spatula, transfer the smelt to a plate or platter covered with paper towels. Keep warm while you cook the remaining smelt.

2 Transfer the fish to a warmed platter and sprinkle with the salt and pepper. Serve hot with the rouille and lemon wedges.

Serves 4

White Bean Soup with Meyer Lemon

Dried beans all have distinctive flavors, but the big white ones are particular favorites. The large Italian butter beans known as Spagna have a particularly robust, meaty flavor. Meyer lemon zest adds a winter citrus note. Wild arugula is a relative of cultivated arugula with deeply indented leaves and a spicy, nutty flavor.

2 cups (about 1 pound) Spagna or other dried large white beans

2 quarts plus 1 cup water

2 teaspoons sea or kosher salt

1 dried bay leaf, or 2 fresh bay leaves

1 fresh rosemary sprig

2 teaspoons freshly ground black pepper

30 wild or small cultivated arugula leaves, coarse stems removed

2½ tablespoons coarsely chopped Meyer lemon zest (from about 2 lemons)

1 Rinse the beans well. In a large pot over high heat, combine the water, beans, salt, bay leaf, and rosemary and bring to a boil. Reduce the heat to low, cover, and simmer, stirring from time to time, until the beans are tender to the bite and the liquid has reduced by half, about 2 hours. Add the pepper and taste, adding more salt if desired.

2 Ladle into warmed bowls, garnish with the arugula leaves and lemon zest, and serve immediately.

Serves 6 to 8

Wonton Soup with Asian Greens

There is a plethora of Asian greens available from different vendors at the market, but the Vue Family Farm specializes in them. If you pick up an unfamiliar green, ask Song or Jer Vue how to cook it. Most likely you will get a demonstration that will give you enough courage to go home and try it yourself. For this recipe, we chose the familiar baby bok choy, but virtually any Asian green or combination of greens can be used.

Soup

3 tablespoons toasted sesame oil

2 tablespoons peeled and minced fresh ginger

1 cup roughly chopped green onions, white and tender green (about ½ inch long)

2 quarts chicken stock, homemade (page 48) or purchased

2 cups sliced baby bok choy (4 or 5 heads, about 8 ounces)

Wontons

10 ounces ground pork

2 tablespoons minced garlic

1½ tablespoons peeled and minced fresh ginger

1 green onion, white and tender green, minced

8 water chestnuts, minced

1½ teaspoons rice vinegar

2 teaspoons tamari or other Japanese soy sauce

2 quarts plus 2 cups water

All-purpose flour for dusting (optional)

1 (4-ounce) package wonton wrappers, about 3 inches square

1. To make the soup, in a soup pot over medium-high heat, warm the sesame oil. When it is hot, add the ginger and sauté, stirring frequently, for 2 minutes. Add the green onions and stock, cover, reduce the heat to low, and simmer for 30 minutes to blend the flavors. Reserve off the heat.

2. To make the wontons, in a bowl, combine the pork, garlic, ginger, green onion, water chestnuts, vinegar, and soy sauce and mix well. Set aside.

3. In a large saucepan over medium-high heat, bring the water to a boil. Turn off the heat.

4. Line a tray with parchment paper or coat it lightly with flour. Set aside.

5. Place a wonton wrapper on a work surface. Keep the remaining wrappers covered with a towel to prevent them from drying out. Place $1/2$ to $3/4$ teaspoon of the pork mixture in the center of the wrapper. With a wet fingertip, moisten the edge of the wrapper on all four sides. Fold the wrapper in half corner to corner to make a triangle, and press down on the edges to seal securely. With a wet fingertip, moisten the two corners on the long side of the triangle (the hypotenuse), fold one to the other, and press together to create a "purse" shape. Place the wonton on the prepared tray and cover with a damp kitchen towel. Repeat until all of the filling is used up. You should have 30 to 36 wontons.

6. Bring the soup base to a boil over medium-high heat. Add the bok choy and reduce the heat to low.

7. Return the saucepan of water to a boil over medium-high heat. Add several of the wontons to the boiling water and cook for 2 minutes exactly. The wrappers should be just tender and the filling cooked through. As the wontons are cooked, scoop them out with a wire skimmer and place 3 or 4 in each bowl. Repeat until all of the wontons are cooked.

8. Ladle the hot soup over the wontons in each bowl. Serve right away.

Serves 8

Radicchio Salad with Blood Oranges

Radicchio is the staple winter salad of Italy, where it fills marketplaces and is on almost every menu. While traveling there one winter, seeking out vegetable varieties for Le Marché Seeds, I visited the sandy commercial radicchio fields outside Chioggia, not far from the Adriatic. My Italian hosts, after taking me on a tour through a warehouse filled with bins and bins of radicchio, took me to lunch and made sure I ordered a radicchio salad, not unlike this one.

1 head radicchio

2 blood oranges, peeled, segmented, and seeds removed

2 tablespoons fresh blood orange juice

1 tablespoon sherry vinegar

3 tablespoons extra-virgin olive oil

¼ teaspoon coarse sea or kosher salt

¼ teaspoon freshly ground black pepper

½ cup young arugula leaves

2-ounce chunk Parmesan cheese

1 Trim the radicchio of any discolored outer leaves and discard them. Tear the head into bite-size pieces, enough to make 2 cups. Cut the orange segments in half and set aside.

2 In the bottom of a salad bowl, combine the blood orange juice, vinegar, olive oil, salt, and pepper and mix well with a fork. Add the radicchio, arugula, and orange pieces. Turn gently to mix. Divide evenly among 4 salad plates. Using a vegetable peeler, shave about 12 thin curls from the chunk of Parmesan and divide them evenly among the salads. Reserve the remaining cheese for another use. Serve the salads at once.

Serves 4

Tomato Aspic with Green Goddess Dressing

It may seem strange to find a tomato recipe in the chapter for winter, when tomatoes are out of season, but homemade tomato sauce, which is cooked down to the very essence of tomatoes, makes the best base for tomato aspic, which, like Devils on Horseback (page 189), is a retro dish that is making a comeback. Served with homemade green goddess dressing and a wedge of crunchy Little Gem lettuce, this aspic is a sublime taste of the winter and the summer market.

3 to 3¼ cups Summer Tomato Sauce (page 136), or 2 cups tomato juice and 1 cup canned tomatoes with their juice, crushed

½ teaspoon sea or kosher salt

¼ teaspoon paprika

⅛ teaspoon cayenne pepper

2 tablespoons fresh lemon juice

¼ cup chopped white onion

4 celery stalks, chopped

2 envelopes (about 2½ teaspoons each) powdered gelatin

¼ cup cold water

4 heads Little Gem or hearts of romaine, halved

Dressing

1 cup mayonnaise

½ cup sour cream

3 anchovy fillets, minced

1 clove garlic, minced

½ cup minced fresh chives

¼ cup minced fresh flat-leaf parsley

2 tablespoons minced fresh tarragon

1 tablespoon fresh lemon juice

1 tablespoon Champagne vinegar

½ teaspoon sea or kosher salt

¼ teaspoon freshly ground black pepper

1. In a saucepan over medium heat, warm the tomato sauce until it is simmering. Increase the heat to medium-high, add the salt, paprika, cayenne pepper, lemon juice, onion, and celery, and bring to a boil. Reduce the heat to very low, cover, and simmer until the flavors have blended, about 30 minutes.

2. Remove from the heat and strain through a chinois or a fine-mesh sieve, pushing it through to get all of the juice.

3. In a small bowl, sprinkle the gelatin over the water and let sit for 3 minutes to soften. Add the water to the still-hot tomato mixture and stir slowly to dissolve the gelatin, 1 to 2 minutes.

4. Line an 8½-by-4½-inch loaf pan or similar-size mold with plastic wrap, smoothing any wrinkles and allowing the plastic wrap to overhang the edges by a few inches. The plastic wrap helps when it comes time to unmold the gelatin. Pour the tomato sauce into the mold, cover with the overhanging plastic wrap, and refrigerate until set, at least 6 hours or up to overnight.

5. To make the dressing, in a bowl, combine all of the ingredients and mix well. You should have about 1⅔ cups. Cover and refrigerate until serving.

6. To unmold the aspic, dip the bottom of the pan in about ½ inch hot water for about 30 seconds. Invert a plate over the mold and, holding the plate and mold together, invert them so the aspic drops onto the plate. Lift off the pan and peel off the plastic wrap.

7. To serve, cut the aspic into 1-inch-thick slices. Place a lettuce half on each salad plate. Place a slice of aspic alongside each lettuce half and finish with a dollop of the dressing.

Serves 8

Tempura Vegetables with Shredded Daikon Dipping Sauce

Georgeanne insisted tempura was easy to make, so I decided to give it a try with a young friend. We produced an airy batter, dipped our vegetables into it, and then fried them until the batter was puffed and golden. After snacking on a few while we cooked, we sat down to eat the remainder. If you want your guests to savor the tempura at its prime, cook and serve it immediately, right out of the pan, rather than waiting until all of the vegetables are cooked.

Winter vegetables are suggested here, but tempura can be made in any season using whatever is available at the market. You can substitute all-purpose flour for the cake flour, but the latter makes a lighter batter.

Dipping Sauce

1 cup water

½ cup tamari or other Japanese soy sauce

⅓ cup mirin (sweet Japanese cooking wine)

2 tablespoons peeled and minced fresh ginger

1 daikon radish, peeled and finely grated (about 3 cups)

Vegetables

Florets from 1 bunch broccoli

3 carrots, peeled and sliced on the diagonal ¼ to ½ inch thick

2 potatoes, peeled and cut into slices ¼ to ½ inch thick

2 yams, peeled and sliced on the diagonal ¼ to ½ inch thick

8 to 10 cultivated brown or white button mushrooms, stems removed

½ cup cake flour or all-purpose flour

Batter

1 egg

½ cup ice-cold water

1 cup cake flour or all-purpose flour

½ teaspoon sea or kosher salt

Canola or other light vegetable oil for deep-frying

1 To make the dipping sauce, in a small bowl, combine the water, soy sauce, mirin, and ginger and mix well. Let sit for at least 30 minutes before serving.

2 To ready the vegetables, pat all of them dry with paper towels. Spread the flour in a shallow bowl. Reserve the vegetables and flour.

3 To make the batter, in a bowl, whisk the egg until blended, then whisk in the ice water. Add the flour and salt and stir to combine, mixing as little as possible so that the batter remains light.

4 Pour the oil to a depth of 3 inches into a deep, wide, heavy pan and heat over medium-high heat. The oil is ready when it registers 340° to 360°F on a deep-frying thermometer, or when a small amount of the batter dropped into the pan stops midway into the oil and then gradually rises up. If the batter sinks, the oil is not hot enough. If it rises immediately, the oil is too hot.

5 Using tongs, dredge a vegetable in the flour, then swirl it in the batter, coating it very lightly. Shake off the excess batter and place the vegetable in the oil. Working quickly, dredge and coat more vegetables the same way, being careful not to crowd the pan. Cook, turning once, until the edges barely turn golden, about 1 minute total. Using the tongs, transfer the vegetables to a platter or plate lined with paper towels. Taste the first few vegetables. They should be slightly crunchy but not taste raw. If they do taste raw, cook subsequent batches a little longer.

6 Place the tempura on a platter and serve. Divide the dipping sauce among individual sauce bowls and put the daikon in a separate bowl to be added to the sauce as desired by the diners.

Serves 8 to 10 as a side dish or 4 to 6 as a main dish

Cracked Dungeness Crab

As soon as the season starts, usually in November, Ann and I rush out to buy locally caught Dungeness crabs. They are available at the market freshly cooked, or you can preorder live crabs. A couple of winters ago, we even went crabbing for our own, outfitted with nets and with bait that proved to be attractive only to the seals. Crabs can be sold "ocean run," which are mixed sizes, or graded, with select grade running more than two pounds. Using uniform-size crabs is best because they cook in the same amount of time.

3 tablespoons sea or kosher salt

½ lemon, 1 bay leaf, and a combination of 1 tablespoon mustard seeds, 2 teaspoons coriander seeds, 2 teaspoons dill seeds, and 1 teaspoon red pepper flakes per crab (optional)

1 or 2 live Dungeness crabs, 1½ pounds or more each

Large pan or bucket of ice water

For Serving

Melted unsalted butter for serving with room-temperature crab

Lemon wedges; horseradish sauce; or mayonnaise flavored to taste with lemon juice, Worcestershire sauce, ketchup, and cayenne pepper for serving with chilled crab

1. Bring a large pot two-thirds full of water to a boil over medium-high heat and add the salt. If you want the crab(s) spicy, add the lemon, bay leaf, and spices. Drop in the crab(s), bring the water back to a boil, reduce the heat to medium, and keep at a strong boil for 20 to 25 minutes. Unfortunately there is not a good visual cue for when a crab is done, so set your timer, cooking the longer time if using large crab(s). Watch the pot so the foam doesn't overflow. Remove the crab(s) and plunge into the ice water until cool.

2. Twist off the legs at the joint closest to the body. Set the legs aside. Place the crab on its back and, with the heels of your hands, press down on each side of the shell until it cracks down the center. Pull off each half shell, then pry up and break off the tail piece and discard. Pull off the mandibles around the mouth and discard. Turn the body over and clean off the spongy gill—dead man's fingers—and discard. Rinse the body well under

3. cold running water and break it into serving pieces. Arrange on a platter. With a crab cracker or nutcracker, crack the center of each segment of the legs and claws, then add to the platter with the body.

   Serve the cracked crab at room temperature with melted butter, or chill the crab and serve cold with lemon wedges, horseradish sauce, or flavored mayonnaise.

1 medium crab serves 1 or 2

Savoy Cabbage Rolls Stuffed with Mushrooms and Pork

Huge heads of ruffled-leaved Savoy cabbage are among the most beautiful vegetables at the market in winter. They inspire memories of the stuffed cabbage rolls made by my neighbor in Provence, well filled and baked with a thin covering of her homemade tomato sauce. This is my version of her dish. If you don't have homemade sauce on hand, like the sauce Ann and I make (see page 136), use the recipe below. These stuffed rolls make a festive and colorful dish that can feed a crowd.

Sauce

- 1 tablespoon extra-virgin olive oil
- 2 tablespoons minced shallot
- 2 cups canned tomatoes, chopped, with their juice
- 1 teaspoon fresh thyme leaves
- Sea or kosher salt and freshly ground black pepper

Stuffing

- 1 cup whole milk
- 6 to 8 ciabatta or other coarse country bread slices, crusts removed
- Sea or kosher salt
- 20 tender inner leaves from about 2 heads Savoy cabbage, with outer leaves reserved
- 2 tablespoons unsalted butter, plus more if needed
- 1 yellow onion, minced
- 1 pound pork fillet, finely chopped
- 1 pound cultivated white or brown mushrooms, finely chopped
- ¼ cup chopped fresh flat-leaf parsley
- 2 tablespoons chopped fresh thyme
- ½ teaspoon freshly ground black pepper
- Canola or other light vegetable oil for the baking dish

1 To make the sauce, in a saucepan over medium-high heat, warm the olive oil. When it is hot, add the shallot and sauté until translucent, 2 to 3 minutes. Add the tomatoes and their juice and the thyme and bring to a boil. Reduce the heat to medium and cook, stirring occasionally, until a sauce has formed, about 20 minutes. Season with salt and pepper and remove from the heat. You should have about 1½ cups.

2 To make the stuffing, in a bowl, combine the milk and bread and let stand until the bread is soft and the milk can be squeezed out, about 10 minutes, depending on how dry the bread is.

3 Meanwhile, bring a large pot of water to a boil over medium heat. Add 1 teaspoon salt and the 20 inner cabbage leaves and blanch until bright green and limp, about 2 minutes. Scoop them out of the water with a wire skimmer, lay them flat on dry towels, and reserve. Return the water to a boil over medium heat, add the outer leaves, and blanch the same way. Scoop them out of the water and pat them dry. Reserve 4 or 5 whole outer leaves. Finely chop the remaining outer leaves; you should have 1½ cups. Set aside.

4 In a large sauté pan over medium heat, melt the butter. When it foams, add the onion and pork and sauté, stirring often, just until the onion and pork are lightly golden, about 5 minutes. Using a slotted spoon, transfer to a bowl and set aside. Return the pan to medium heat and add the mushrooms, adding more butter if the pan seems dry. Sauté until the mushrooms are golden and have released their juices, about 5 minutes.

5 In a large bowl, combine the meat mixture and mushrooms. Squeeze the bread to release the excess milk, then tear it into small pieces and add it to the bowl along with the chopped cabbage leaves, parsley, thyme, 1 teaspoon salt, and the pepper. Taste and adjust the seasoning if needed.

6 Preheat the oven to 350°F. Lightly oil a 9-by-16-inch or similar-size baking dish.

7 Lay a blanched inner cabbage leaf, cupped side up, on a work surface. Place a ball of filling about the size of small egg near the center of the leaf and about an inch from the stem end. The amount of filling you use will depend on the size of the leaf. Fold the stem end over the filling, fold in the sides, and then fold down the top, envelope style. Place the roll, seam side down, in the prepared dish. Repeat with the remaining blanched inner leaves and the filling, packing the rolls snugly in the baking dish.

8 When all of the rolls are in the dish, spoon the sauce evenly over the top. Arrange the reserved blanched outer leaves over the rolls, covering them completely, then cover the dish with aluminum foil. Bake until the stuffing is fully cooked and the rolls are tender, about 45 minutes.

9 To serve, remove and discard the foil and the whole cabbage leaves. Serve the rolls piping hot directly from the dish.

Serves 8 to 10

Pork Rib Roast, Tuscan Style

For a drop-dead, knock-your-socks-off centerpiece meal that commands attention and anticipation, this is the dish to serve. It is visually dramatic and packed with the big, bold flavors of rural Tuscany. At the market, this special cut needs to be preordered from Bledsoe Purebred. Ann and I have both made and served this dish on several occasions, and I, at least, save the bones to gnaw on. Don't trim off the fat before roasting, as it is the fat that slowly bastes the meat as it cooks. The roast goes well with winter vegetables such as braised Brussels sprouts, chard, or broccoli and with mashed potatoes or celery root to soak up the juices.

3 tablespoons fennel seeds

1 bone-in pork loin, about 8 pounds

1 large head garlic, cloves separated and minced

Zest of 3 lemons, minced

2 tablespoons sea or kosher salt

1 tablespoon freshly ground black pepper

5 tablespoons coarsely chopped fresh rosemary

1 tablespoon unsalted butter

1. Preheat the oven to 375°F.

2. In a small, dry frying pan over low heat, toast the fennel seeds, shaking the pan occasionally, until fragrant, about 3 minutes. Let cool, then finely grind in a spice grinder or with a mortar and pestle. Set aside.

3. Slip a long, sharp knife right next to the rack of bones at one end of the roast and run the blade along the bones, slicing through to separate the bones from the meat. Keep the bones intact because they will be retied onto the roast. Set the bones aside.

4. Rub the garlic onto the meat exposed by the removal of the bones, covering it fully with a layer of garlic. Then, top the garlic layer with a layer of the lemon zest. Sprinkle with half of the salt, then half of the pepper, and finally with all of the rosemary and fennel seed. Using cotton string, tie the bones back onto the loin. Rub the roast with the remaining salt and pepper.

5 Place the roast, fat side up, in a roasting pan and roast until golden brown and an instant-read thermometer inserted into the thickest part of the loin without touching bone registers just short of 140°F, about 1½ hours. Transfer the roast to a carving board, snip the string, and remove the rack of bones. Cover the roast loosely with aluminum foil and let rest for 15 to 20 minutes. Reserve the juices in the roasting pan for the pan sauce. Increase the oven temperature to 450°F.

6 To roast the bones, increase the oven temperature to 450°F. Put the bones in a clean roasting pan, place in the oven, and roast until crispy, about 15 minutes. Just before the bones are ready, make the pan sauce. Add any juices captured on the carving board to the roasting pan, skim off the fat with a large spoon, and place the pan over medium heat. Add the butter and stir until melted and smooth.

7 To serve, carve the roast into slices about ½ inch thick and arrange on a warmed platter. Cut the rack of bones apart into single bones and arrange on the platter with the slices. Pour a little of the sauce over each slice and serve immediately.

Serves 10

Oven-Roasted Brussels Sprouts with Thyme Butter

Brussels sprouts, which thrive in the cool climate of California's Central Coast, often arrive at the market on their stalks. Roasting the sprouts develops a sweet flavor. For an extra-rich dish, roast heads of garlic at the same time, then squeeze out the carmelized cloves and mix them with the Brussel sprouts.

2 pounds Brussels sprouts, stems trimmed and rough outer leaves removed

2 heads garlic (optional)

2 or 3 tablespoons extra-virgin olive oil

4 tablespoons unsalted butter, at room temperature

1 tablespoon fresh thyme leaves

½ teaspoon sea or kosher salt

½ teaspoon freshly cracked black pepper

1. Preheat the oven to 400°F.

2. Place the Brussels sprouts in a single layer in a shallow baking dish. If using the garlic heads, cut off the top ½ inch from each head to expose the cloves and add the heads to the dish. Drizzle the sprouts with 2 tablespoons olive oil, or drizzle the sprouts and garlic with 3 tablespoons olive oil. Turn to coat evenly, then sprinkle with the salt and pepper.

3. Roast, stirring every 5 to 10 minutes, until the sprouts have some golden color, about 40 minutes. If roasting garlic heads, they should give a little to the touch.

4. Meanwhile, in a small bowl, mash the butter. Add the thyme and mix thoroughly. Set aside.

5. When the sprouts are ready, remove the dish from the oven. If you have roasted garlic heads, remove them from the dish and let them cool until they can be handled. Remove the garlic cloves from their skins by gently squeezing each clove. Transfer the sprouts to a serving dish, add the garlic cloves, and stir to combine. Add the thyme butter and stir just to coat the Brussels sprouts with the butter. Serve at once.

Serves 4 to 6

California Lime Pie

Pie is my favorite dessert, and though Georgeanne loves cherry pie, California lime is my all-time favorite. California limes are less tart than Key limes, so more juice is required. When I created this pie crust, it reminded me of crusts that I have eaten with a custard or a banana cream filling: not flaky, rather sturdy, a bit crumbly, and almost light and crispy, like shortbread. It perfectly suits a single-crust pie with a cooked filling, like this one. For fruit pies, I prefer a flakier crust (see page 45).

Crust	Filling
2½ cups all-purpose flour	5 egg yolks
1 teaspoon sea or kosher salt	1 can (14 ounces) sweetened condensed milk
1 cup (2 cubes) unsalted butter, frozen and cut into walnut-size pieces	4 to 5 limes
5 tablespoons ice-cold water	1 cup heavy cream
	2 tablespoons confectioners' sugar

1. To make the crust, in a food processor, combine the flour and salt and pulse several times to mix. Scatter the butter over the flour mixture and pulse five to seven times, until the butter is in pea-size balls and covered with flour. Add the ice water all at once and, using ½-second pulses, pulse about five times, just until the water is incorporated and the dough comes together in a rough mass. Do not overwork the dough or the gluten in the flour will develop and the crust will be tough.

2. Divide the dough in half and shape each half into a firm ball. Lightly dust the balls with flour, and then flatten each ball into a thick disk. Cover each disk with plastic wrap. You will need only a single disk for this recipe. Place it in the refrigerator for 30 minutes or in the freezer for 10 minutes. Reserve the remaining disk for another use it. It will keep in the refrigerator for up to 1 week and in the freezer for up to 1 month. If frozen, thaw overnight in the refrigerator. Meanwhile, preheat the oven to 425°F.

3. On a lightly floured work surface, roll out the dough into a 12-inch round (to fit a 10-inch pie pan) about 1/3 inch thick, moving and flouring the disk two or three times to avoid sticking, handling the dough as little as possible, and working quickly so the dough remains cool. Place the rolling pin on the far edge of the round and roll the crust up onto the pin. Position the pin over a 10-inch pie pan and unroll the dough round, centering it over the pan. Press it into the bottom and sides of the pan. Trim the edge so that you have a 1-inch overhang, then fold the overhang under and flute the edge. Line the pastry with a sheet of aluminum foil, pressing it against the sides and bottom of the pan, and fill with pie weights or dried beans.

4. Bake until the edges begin to turn lightly golden, about 6 minutes. Remove the weights and foil, prick the bottom in several places with the tines of a fork, and continue to bake until the bottom is lightly golden, about 4 minutes longer. Transfer to a wire rack and let cool completely. Reduce the oven temperature to 350°F.

5. To make the filling, in a large bowl, whisk the egg yolks just until blended. Stir in the sweetened condensed milk. Grate the zest of 1 lime and set aside. Juice the limes until you have 3/4 cup juice. Stir the lime juice, 1 to 2 tablespoons at a time, into the yolk mixture.

6. Pour the filling into the prebaked pie shell. Bake until the filling is firm, about 15 minutes. Let cool completely on a wire rack.

7. In a bowl, using an electric mixer, beat the cream on medium-high speed until soft peaks form, 3 to 4 minutes. Add the sugar and continue to beat on medium-high speed until stiff peaks form, about 4 minutes longer. Cover and refrigerate until serving.

8. Spread the whipped cream over the cooled lime filling. Sprinkle the cream with the reserved lime zest. Serve at room temperature if serving within 3 hours, or cover and refrigerate for up to 1 day, then bring to room temperature before serving.

Serves 8 to 10

Navel Oranges with Lavender Syrup

Joan Gussow, a radical nutritionist whom I admire, once described oranges as perfectly packaged because when you peel them the peel is useful or biodegradable and a beautiful fragrance fills the air. That fragrance can be discerned in the market when oranges are in full season. When I make this dessert, I sometimes dry the leftover orange peels for use in stews or I use them fresh in marmalade (see page 227). Georgeanne and I also candy them (see page 229).

Lavender Syrup

4 cups water

2 cups sugar

2 tablespoons dried lavender flowers, or ½ cup fresh lavender flowers

10 navel oranges, peeled and sliced crosswise ¼ inch thick

1. To make the syrup, in a saucepan over medium-high heat, combine the water and sugar and bring to a boil, stirring to dissolve the sugar. Reduce the heat to medium and simmer, continuing to stir, until the sugar dissolves and a thin syrup forms, about 10 minutes. Remove from the heat, add the lavender, cover, and let stand overnight in a cool place.

2. Strain the syrup through a chinois or a colander lined with triple-layered cheesecloth. Discard the lavender. Measure ⅓ cup syrup and set aside to use with the oranges. Transfer the remaining syrup to a dry, sterilized bottle, seal with a cork, and store in a cool, dark place. It will keep for at least 3 months.

3. Arrange the orange slices on a platter and drizzle with the lavender syrup. Serve at room temperature or chilled.

Serves 10 to 12

Pears with Blue Cheese, Walnuts, and Honey

Pears, blue cheese, and walnuts are a traditional dessert trio, and here we've given that classic a twist by roasting the pears. Remember, pears ripen off the tree, so buy them a few days before you plan to use them and set them out on your kitchen counter to ripen. Roasting them slowly with butter intensifies their natural buttery flavor and helps to cook them to juicy spoon-softness. Drizzling them with honey from McDonald Orchards, a longtime market vendor, is the final touch.

4 pears, halved and cored

2 tablespoons unsalted butter, melted

4 to 6 ounces blue cheese

2 tablespoons chopped walnuts

8 tablespoons honey

1. Preheat the oven to 350°F.

2. Using a pastry brush, brush the butter over the pear halves, both skin and cut side. Put the pear halves, cut side down, in a baking dish just large enough to accommodate them.

3. Bake the pears until tender to a fork, about 20 minutes. Remove from the oven, turn the pears over, and dab a spoonful of the blue cheese in the center of each pear half. Sprinkle the pears evenly with the walnuts, return the dish to the oven, and bake until the cheese is warm, 2 to 3 minutes.

4. Transfer the pears to individual plates, drizzle with honey, and serve warm.

Serves 8

Three Citrus Thick-Cut Marmalade

This is a marmalade lover's marmalade. I first made it for my husband, David, who was homesick for English marmalade and because a bad frost that year meant that the oranges on our tree needed to be used quickly. Combining navel oranges, which are much sweeter than the bitter Seville oranges used in traditional English marmalade, with tart lemons and a grapefruit helps to produce marmalade reminiscent of one made with Sevilles.

You will need four pint canning jars with lids and rings, a large canning kettle with a rack and cover (or a large, wide pot with a wire rack and cover) for the water bath, a large, heavy nonreactive pot for cooking the marmalade, canning tongs, and a ladle.

3 large navel oranges	2 quarts plus 3 cups water
2 large or 3 small lemons	8 cups sugar
1 grapefruit	

1 Quarter the oranges, lemons, and grapefruit through the stem end. Place the cut fruits in a large glass bowl or other nonreactive container, add the water, and let stand overnight.

2 The next day, remove the fruit from the water and cut each citrus quarter crosswise into 1/8-inch-thick slices. Transfer the fruit slices to the large, heavy nonreactive pot and add the soaking water. Place over medium-high heat, bring to a boil, and boil uncovered, stirring occasionally to prevent scorching, for 1 hour.

3 Meanwhile, set up the water bath. Fill the canning kettle with water (the water must be deep enough to cover the jars by 1 to 2 inches) and bring to a boil over high heat. If you don't have a canning kettle, use a large, wide pot and put a wire rack in the bottom of the pot before you fill it with water. Once the water boils, you can turn off the heat and then return it to a boil just before you put the jars in the kettle.

4. Wash the canning jars in hot, soapy water and rinse well. Place the jars in a saucepan, add water to cover generously, and bring to a boil over medium-high heat. Boil for 15 minutes, then turn off the heat and leave the jars in the hot water until you are ready to fill them. Fill another saucepan half full with water and bring to a boil over medium-high heat. Add the canning lids and rings and boil for 5 minutes. Turn off the heat and leave the lids and rings in the hot water until needed.

5. When the citrus has boiled for 1 hour, add the sugar, stir until dissolved, and then continue to boil until the mixture registers 220°F on a candy thermometer, 20 to 40 minutes. After 20 minutes, you will notice the color change to deep amber. As the temperature of the mixture rises, the boil changes from a slow boil with large bubbles to a rapid boil with very small bubbles.

6. Just before the marmalade is ready, using tongs, transfer the jars to a work surface. Return the water in the canning kettle to a boil. Ladle the hot marmalade into the hot, sterilized jars, filling them to within 1/2 inch of the rim. With a clean, damp cloth, wipe the rim of each jar. Place a lid on the rim and then screw on a ring, being careful not to screw it on too tightly. Put the filled jars into the rack of the canner and lower the rack into the boiling water. If you are using a large, wide pot, use the canning tongs to lower the jars onto the rack in the bottom of the pot, making sure the jars do not touch. Return the water to a rolling boil, reduce the heat slightly, cover, and boil for 5 minutes.

7. Cover a work surface with a folded towel. Using the canning tongs, transfer the jars to the towel, spacing them a few inches apart. As the jars begin to cool, you may hear popping sounds, which is the sound of the lids sealing. The lids should be indented. When the jars are completely cool, after at least 12 hours, check the seal on each jar by pressing on the center of the lid. If it remains indented, the seal is good. If it does not, refrigerate the jar and use the marmalade within 1 month.

8. Label the jars with the contents and date and store in a cool, dry place for up to 1 year.

Makes 4 pints

Candied Orange or Lemon Peel

These are festive holiday candies made from winter's fruit. They make sweet yet tart additions to salads and to ice cream, chocolate cake, or other desserts. The last of the Valencia oranges are the best choice here, as they most resemble the bitter Seville oranges probably used in the original English recipe. Navel oranges will suffice if you don't have Valencias. Use Lisbon or Eureka lemons, as the peel of the Meyer lemon is too thin.

3 lemons or oranges

3 quarts plus 2 cups water

1½ cups sugar

1 Cut a thin slice from the top and bottom of each fruit, then cut vertically through the peel to the fruit, spacing the cuts about 1 inch apart. Remove the peel from each fruit. Reserve the fruit for another use.

2 If you are using the peel to make a candy instead of chopping it, cut each peel section lengthwise into strips ¼ inch wide. If you will be chopping it, leave the peel sections whole, as they are easier to work with.

3 In a saucepan, combine 3 quarts of the water and the peel over high heat and bring to a boil. Reduce the heat to medium and cook, uncovered, until only 1 inch or so of the water remains in the pan, about 1 hour. Using a slotted spoon, transfer the peels to a bowl and set aside. Discard the liquid.

4 In a nonreactive saucepan, combine the remaining 2 cups water with 1 cup of the sugar and bring to a boil over high heat, stirring until the sugar dissolves. Remove from the heat and stir the still-warm peels into the syrup. Let the peels stand for 1 to 2 hours at room temperature. Return the pan to low heat and cook the peels, stirring occasionally, until they have absorbed all of the syrup, about 30 minutes. The peels will become translucent and amber. During the last stages of cooking, keep a close eye on the peels to prevent scorching.

5 When the peels are ready, remove the pan from the heat and transfer the peels to a sheet of waxed paper or parchment paper, arranging them in a single layer. Let them dry overnight. To sugar them, place the remaining ½ cup sugar on a fresh piece of waxed paper or parchment and roll the fruit in it, adding more sugar if needed. Let stand overnight.

6 Transfer to an airtight container and store in a dry place for up to 2 weeks.

Makes about 4 ounces

JANET WAGNER, CEO OF SUTTER DAVIS HOSPITAL, BUYS FARM-FRESH VEGETABLES FROM A LOCAL FARMER AT THE SUTTER DAVIS HOSPITAL FARMERS MARKET.

FARMERS' MARKETS FOR HEALTH: SUTTER DAVIS HOSPITAL

At Sutter Davis Hospital, we are committed to improving public health both inside and outside our walls. All experts agree that good health begins with farm-fresh food, and we want to be the healthcare leaders in improving patient care, health, and well-being.

The Davis Farmers Market Cookbook provides area residents with simple and easy ways to incorporate seasonal fruits and vegetables into their meal plans. Award-winning cookbook author Georgeanne Brennan and former Davis mayor Ann Evans have teamed up to assemble recipes that are not only accessible but that also reflect well-balanced meals using food products grown and raised locally.

Sponsoring the Davis Farmers Market is just one additional way Sutter Davis Hospital hopes to achieve our mission of improving the lives of the people in our community. In 2010, Davis Farmers Market and Sutter Davis Hospital began their partnership to promote healthy eating under the slogan "Good Health Begins with Farm-Fresh Food." The increase in type 2 diabetes, heart disease, and childhood obesity in communities across the country make partnerships like this one particularly important.

At Sutter Davis Hospital, we passionately believe that eating fresh fruits and vegetables is central to overall health. The weekly, seasonal Sutter Davis Hospital Farmers Market, in partnership with the Davis Farmers Market, is the first farmers market in the country affiliated with a hospital. We believe that this unique on-site market gives our staff and the people of the community the information and ability to make healthy choices that positively impact their bodies and the community they live in by supporting local farmers. Serving and selling locally grown food with high nutritional value at a hospital just makes good sense.

Prevention is also a critical part of the practice of medicine, and having a focus on overall well-being, eating right, and exercising daily is beneficial to people of all ages. That's why Sutter Davis Hospital also works closely with the Davis Farmers Market Foundation to support Davis Farm to School, a program that supports the Davis Joint Unified School District in its goal of increasing farm-fresh foods in school meals. Farm to School programs provide educational opportunities to students through garden-based learning, local farm visits, and comprehensive recycling programs. They introduce children to farm-fresh food at a young age and train their palates so they will make healthier choices as they grow, which is essential in maintaining lifelong health.

Sutter Davis Hospital stands behind the community of Davis and the organizations that support making healthy choices. It is our hope that these efforts can make a significant impact on the growing health of our community. As a proud partner of the Davis Farmers Market and its Foundation, Sutter Davis Hospital is thrilled with the publication of *The Davis Farmers Market Cookbook*.

— Janet Wagner
CEO, Sutter Davis Hospital

Acknowledgments

The Market

First, we want to thank the board members of the Davis Farmers Market Association for trusting us to write the cookbook that reflects the history and values of the market. We commend them for their desire to have the book printed domestically and for securing the special funding from their partner, Sutter Davis Hospital, to underwrite that additional cost.

A special thanks to Rich Collins, chair, and Jim Eldon, treasurer, for their help and ongoing support and enthusiasm. Longtime board member Steve Smit provided encouragement with his interest in the book's progress when we shopped with him on Saturday mornings.

Randii MacNear, market manager, for her immediate positive response when we first presented our dream of this project to her in Ann's living room; for her help throughout the process, including the wonderful group farmers' photo; and for her great marketing ideas. Her leadership works magic at the market, as she expands it to other venues in Davis and other towns and continues to shepherd its growth, without sacrificing intimacy, in Central Park.

Shelly Keller for her belief in the importance of this book to the market and the community and for her stellar planning and publicity.

And to all of the farmers and vendors at the market who welcomed our photographer Craig Lee into their market world and onto their farms, including Thad Barsotti, John Bledsoe, Rich Collins, Jim Eldon, Dianne and Mike Madison, Michael McDonald, Karen and Scott Stone, Carol Vail, Ed Mehl, and Jeff and Annie Main.

The Team

Craig Lee, photographer, whose project this is as much as it is ours. He has captured the spirit and light of the market and foods throughout the seasons and trekked to the farms to capture the farmers on their land.

Ethel Brennan, photo stylist and art director, who brought her keen professional eye and talent for color and design to the project, and who insisted that her mother have the best.

Kristine Brogno for her wondrous design of the book and cover and for sticking with the team over the two years we have worked on the project.

Sharon Silva, copyeditor, who is without a doubt the cookbook author's best friend. No word, no phrase, no thought is missed by her keen eye. And a special thank you for her early review on our concept of using two voices and for giving it her blessing.

Sharron Wood, proofer, and Amy E. Novick, indexer, who stepped in at the final moments to help conclude the project.

Stephanie Jimenez, our faithful and excellent photo shoot assistant, who started out helping with the cleanup and ended up cooking.

Stephanie Cornejo, who stepped in to assist in a photo shoot at the last minute, doing everything from unloading Ethel's prop-filled station wagon to putting the last dish in the dishwasher.

Special Thanks

Alice Waters, our friend and colleague in different capacities for nearly four decades. We are honored by her heartfelt foreword to our book and applaud all that she does to restore food to its rightful place in a civil society.

Jim Schrupp, an early reader and editor of the book and taster of the recipes, whose eagle eye and good palate helped shape the content.

Joyce Hardi, our bookkeeper, whose ebullient nature creates a supportive environment for us while keeping Evans & Brennan and Mirabelle Press on track.

Especially from Georgeanne

Ann Evans for her friendship, sense of humor, intelligence, and unerring sense of what is the right thing to do.

Bill LeBlond of Chronicle Books for his early interest in the project and his good advice.

Charlotte Kimball, my friend and longtime partner in the extraordinary adventure that was Le Marché Seeds, who taught me so much about horticulture and with whom I first began what has been a long and rewarding career of recipe and food writing.

Tom Schrupp and Katie Chapple and now Silas; Ethel Brennan and Laurent, Oscar, and Raphael Rigobert; Liz Valentine and Oliver, Oona, and Sidney Brennan; Dan Schrupp; Jim Schrupp; and Donald Brennan—my family past and present, of recipe tasters, garden planters, harvesters, and cooks.

Especially from Ann

Georgeanne Brennan for her friendship, her willingness and capacity to help this dream sprout wings, her sage and comforting advice as I went through the ups and downs of recipe writing, and, last but not least, the use of her sunny kitchen for the photo shoots.

Martin Barnes (on a trip here from his home in France), Bob Black (while overlooking the Smith River), Henry Esbenshade (on a phone call from his home in Australia), Isao Fujimoto, Desmond Jolly, Phil Kitchen, Randii MacNear, Annie Main, and John Poorbaugh for allowing me to interview them about their early memories of founding or building the market. Randii MacNear for locating the early archival material on the Davis Farmers Market in the storage unit and trusting me with its keeping while I pored over it. Any omissions or errors in the market story are mine.

Jillian Guernsey for bringing her talent and spending her time with me for two days in my kitchen developing recipes and, in particular, testing the pie crust again and again until we got it just right. We ate a lot of good pie together.

Doug Walter and Julie Cross at the Davis Food Co-op for tracking down details when I needed them in a hurry.

Russell Sydney for writing the early history of California markets in his 2005 booklet, "A History of the Farmers' Market Movement in California, Communities Working for Positive Change."

Jamie Buffington, my friend and pancetta-making teacher, for our monthly cooking adventures in the kitchen in which I laugh and learn a lot.

Mark Francis, partner in CoDesign, for his unerring design sense in putting together the first master plan for the expanded Central Park that became the new home for the Davis Farmers Market, and for his leadership in seeing the design through to completion. Maynard Skinner for his Save Open Space campaign, without which we would not have been able to expand the park.

David Thompson, my loving husband for over thirty years, for eating anything I cook and for getting takeout when I'm too busy organizing or writing about food to put a meal on the table.

a

Aioli, Basil, Grilled Eggplant Sandwich with Grilled Sweet Peppers and, 112–14
appetizers. *See* first courses
Apples, Basic Rustic Sweet Tart Recipe with, 43–44
Apples, Quinces, and Pears, Sautéed, with Whipped Cream, 175
Apricot Jam, 89–90
Apricot Pie, Old-Fashioned, 83–85
Artichokes, Italian Stuffed, 64
arugula
    Radicchio Salad with Blood Oranges, 203
    Roasted Beet Salad with Fresh Cheese, Toasted Pistachios, and Pistachio Oil, 151
    Salad of Early Bitter Greens and Late Cherry Tomatoes, 155
    White Bean Soup with Meyer Lemon, 198
Asian Greens, Wonton Soup with, 200–201
Asian-style pasta with seasonal variations, 34–35
Asparagus, Fresh Rag Pasta with Peas and, 69–71
Aspic, Tomato, with Green Goddess Dressing, 204–6
Avocado, Crab Salad on Belgian Endive Leaves with, 186

b

bacon
    Basic Savory Tart Recipe with Chard, Spinach, and Bacon, 38–40
    Devils on Horseback, 189
    Frisée Salad with Egg and Pancetta, 152–53
    Grilled Fig and Lardon Kebabs, 146–48
Barbecued Short Ribs with Dark Sauce, 119–20
basic recipes and seasonal variations
    Fruit Pie Recipe with Cherries, 45–47
    Gratin Recipe with Broccoli, 36–37
    Pasta Recipe, Asian Style, with Sweet Peppers and Tofu, 34–35
    Pasta Recipe, Italian Style, with Sautéed Onions and Sweet Red Peppers, 32–34
    Risotto Recipe with Four Kinds of Mushrooms, 30–32
    Roasted Vegetables Recipe with Spring Vegetables, 40–41
    Rustic Sweet Tart Recipe with Apples, 43–44
    Savory Tart Recipe with Chard, Spinach, and Bacon, 37–40
    Vegetable Fricassee Recipe with Corn and Sweet Pepper, 42
    Vin Maison, 92
basil
    Classic Soupe au Pistou with Fresh Shelling Beans, 149–50
    Grilled Eggplant Sandwich with Grilled Sweet Peppers and Basil Aioli, 112–14
    Summer Tomato Sauce, 136–38
beans
    Classic Soupe au Pistou with Fresh Shelling Beans, 149–50
    Fava Bean Soup with Pancetta, 63
    White Bean Soup with Meyer Lemon, 198
bean sprouts, *in* Fresh Spring Rolls with Thai Dipping Sauce, 66–67
beef
    Barbecued Short Ribs with Dark Sauce, 119–20
    Beef Stock, 49–50
beets
    Basic Roasted Vegetables Recipe with Spring Vegetables, 41
    Roasted Beet Salad with Fresh Cheese, Toasted Pistachios, and Pistachio Oil, 151
Belgian Endive, Braised, 171
Belgian Endive Leaves with Avocado, Crab Salad on, 186
bell peppers. *See* peppers, sweet
Berries, Old-Fashioned Meringues with, 124–26
Black Cherries in Pinot Noir Gelatin, 86–87
Blood Oranges, Radicchio Salad with, 203
Blue Cheese, Walnuts, and Honey, Pears with, 225
bok choy, *in* Wonton Soup with Asian Greens, 200–201
broccoli
    Basic Gratin Recipe with Broccoli, 36–37
    Tempura Vegetables with Shredded Daikon Dipping Sauce, 207–9
Bruschetta with Ricotta, Dill, and Smoked Salmon, 98
Brussels Sprouts, Oven-Roasted, with Thyme Butter, 219
Butter Cookies with Pistachios, Old-Fashioned, 176–77

c

Cabbage Rolls Stuffed with Mushrooms and Pork, 213–15
Candied Orange or Lemon Peel, 229–30
carrots
    Baked Whole Cod with Ginger, Carrots and Green Onions, 77–78
    Basic Roasted Vegetables Recipe with Spring Vegetables, 41
    Tempura Vegetables with Shredded Daikon Dipping Sauce, 207–9
    Young Lamb with Spring Vegetables, 71–72
Chard, Spinach, and Bacon, Basic Savory Tart Recipe with, 38–40
Cherries, Basic Fruit Pie Recipe with, 45–47
Cherries, Black, in Pinot Noir Gelatin, 86–87
chicken
    Chicken Braised in White Wine with Peas, 74–75
    Chicken Stock, 48–49
    Roast Chicken with 40 Cloves of Garlic, 109–10
Chile Relleno Casserole with Red Sauce, 160–61
Chutney, Fall Fruit, 179–80
Cod with Ginger, Carrots and Green Onions, Baked Whole, 77–78
Collard Greens and Wild Mushrooms, Creamy Grits with, 161–63
condiments. *See* preserved foods
Cookies with Pistachios, Old-Fashioned Butter, 176–77
corn
    Basic Vegetable Fricassee Recipe with Corn and Sweet Pepper, 42
    Old-Fashioned Corn Chowder with Rouille, 99–101
    Sweet Corn and Fresh Oregano Fritters, 102–3
Crab, Cracked Dungeness, 211–12
Crab Salad on Belgian Endive Leaves with Avocado, 186
Crostini, Fried Padrón Peppers with Goat Cheese and, 96
Crostini, Grilled Persimmon, with Farmer Cheese, 144–46
cucumbers
    Dill Pickles, 139–41
    Watermelon, Cucumber, and Heirloom Cherry Tomato Salad, 104

d

Daikon Dipping Sauce, Tempura Vegetables with, 207–9
dates, *in* Devils on Horseback, 189
desserts
    Basic Fruit Pie Recipe with Cherries (and seasonal variations), 45–47
    Basic Rustic Sweet Tart Recipe with Apples (and seasonal variations), 43–44
    Black Cherries in Pinot Noir Gelatin, 86–87
    California Lime Pie, 220–21
    Navel Oranges with Lavender Syrup, 222
    Old-Fashioned Apricot Pie, 83–85
    Old-Fashioned Butter Cookies with Pistachios, 176–77
    Old-Fashioned Meringues with Berries, 124–26
    Pears with Blue Cheese, Walnuts, and Honey, 225
    Persimmon Flan, 173–74
    Roasted Summer Fruits with Ice Cream, 126
    Sautéed Quinces, Apples, and Pears with Whipped Cream, 175
Deviled Eggs with Tarragon, 59
Devils on Horseback, 189
Dill Pickles, 139–41
Dipping Sauce, Shredded Daikon, Tempura Vegetables with, 207–9

Dipping Sauce, Thai, Fresh Spring Rolls with, 66–67
Dried Fruits, Roasted Lamb Shanks with, 165–66
Dungeness Crab, Cracked, 211–12

e

Eggplant Sandwich with Grilled Sweet Peppers and Basil Aioli, Grilled, 112–14
eggs
    Chile Relleno Casserole with Red Sauce, 160–61
    Deviled Eggs with Tarragon, 59
    Frisée Salad with Egg and Pancetta, 152–53
    Warm Leek Salad with Oil-Cured Olives and Eggs, 56–58
Endive, Braised Belgian, 171
Endive Leaves with Avocado, Crab Salad on, 186
escarole, *in* Salad of Early Bitter Greens and Late Cherry Tomatoes, 155

f

fall
    seasonal foods, 25, 143
    Braised Belgian Endive, 171
    Chile Relleno Casserole with Red Sauce, 160–61
    Classic Soupe au Pistou with Fresh Shelling Beans, 149–50
    Creamy Grits with Collard Greens and Wild Mushrooms, 161–63
    Fall Fruit Chutney, 179–80
    Frisée Salad with Egg and Pancetta, 152–53
    fruit pie variations, 45
    Grilled Fig and Lardon Kebabs, 146–48
    Grilled Persimmon Crostini with Farmer Cheese, 144–46
    Grilled Stuffed Squid, 156–58
    Musquée de Provence with New Crop Walnuts, 168
    Old-Fashioned Butter Cookies with Pistachios, 176–77
    pasta variations, 33, 35
    Persimmon Flan, 173–74
    Pomegranate Jelly, 181–82
    Pork Country Sausage, 158–59
    risotto variations, 31
    Roasted Beet Salad with Fresh Cheese, Toasted Pistachios, and Pistachio Oil, 151
    Roasted Lamb Shanks with Dried Fruits, 165–66
    roasted vegetable variations, 40
    rustic sweet tart variations, 43
    Salad of Early Bitter Greens and Late Cherry Tomatoes, 155
    Sautéed Quinces, Apples, and Pears with Whipped Cream, 175
    savory gratin variations, 36
    savory tart variations, 38
    vegetable fricassee variations, 42

Fall Fruit Chutney, 179–80
Farmer Cheese, Grilled Persimmon Crostini with, 144–46
Fava Bean Soup with Pancetta, 63
Feta, Flatbreads with Spring Onions and, 60–62
figs
    Grilled Fig and Lardon Kebabs, 146–48
    Roasted Summer Fruits with Ice Cream, 126
first courses. *See also* salads; soups
    Bruschetta with Ricotta, Dill, and Smoked Salmon, 98
    Deviled Eggs with Tarragon, 59
    Devils on Horseback, 189
    Flatbreads with Spring Onions and Feta, 60–62
    Fresh Spring Rolls with Thai Dipping Sauce, 66–67
    Fried Oyster Sliders with Homemade Tartar Sauce, 195–96
    Fried Padrón Peppers with Goat Cheese and Crostini, 96
    Fried Smelt with Rouille Dipping Sauce, 196
    Grilled Fig and Lardon Kebabs, 146–48
    Grilled Persimmon Crostini with Farmer Cheese, 144–46
    Italian Stuffed Artichokes, 64
    Sweet Corn and Fresh Oregano Fritters, 102–3
fish. *See* seafood
Flan, Green Garlic, 80–82
Flan, Persimmon, 173–74
Flatbreads with Spring Onions and Feta, 60–62
Frisée Salad with Egg and Pancetta, 152–53
Fruit Pie Recipe with Cherries, Basic (and seasonal variations), 45–47

g

Garlic, Roast Chicken with 40 Cloves of, 109–10
Gelatin, Pinot Noir, Black Cherries in, 86–87
Ginger, Carrots and Green Onions, Baked Whole Cod with, 77–78
goat cheese
    Basic Savory Tart Recipe with Chard, Spinach, and Bacon, 38–40
    Fried Padrón Peppers with Goat Cheese and Crostini, 96
    Roasted Beet Salad with Fresh Cheese, Toasted Pistachios, and Pistachio Oil, 151
grapefruit, *in* Three Citrus Thick-Cut Marmalade, 227–28
grapes, *in* Roasted Summer Fruits with Ice Cream, 126
Gratin, Zucchini and Gruyére, 110–11
Gratin Recipe with Broccoli, Basic (and seasonal variations), 36–37

green and spring onions
    Baked Whole Cod with Ginger, Carrots and Green Onions, 77–78
    Chicken Braised in White Wine with Peas, 74–75
    Flatbreads with Spring Onions and Feta, 60–62
    Fresh Spring Rolls with Thai Dipping Sauce, 66–67
    Wonton Soup with Asian Greens, 200–201
green beans, *in* Classic Soupe au Pistou with Fresh Shelling Beans, 149–50
green garlic
    Fresh Spring Rolls with Thai Dipping Sauce, 66–67
    Green Garlic Flan, 80–82
green onions
    Baked Whole Cod with Ginger, Carrots and Green Onions, 77–78
    Chicken Braised in White Wine with Peas, 74–75
    Fresh Spring Rolls with Thai Dipping Sauce, 66–67
    Wonton Soup with Asian Greens, 200–201
Greens, Asian, Wonton Soup with, 200–201
Greens, Early Bitter, and Late Cherry Tomatoes, Salad of, 155
Grits, Creamy, with Collard Greens and Wild Mushrooms, 161–63
Gruyére and Zucchini Gratin, 110–11

i

Ice Cream, Roasted Summer Fruits with, 126
Italian Stuffed Artichokes, 64
Italian-style pasta with seasonal variations, 32–34

j

jams and jellies. *See* preserved foods

k

Kebabs, Grilled Fig and Lardon, 146–48
Ketchup, Homemade, 133–35

l

Lamb, Young, with Spring Vegetables, 71–72
Lamb Shanks with Dried Fruits, Roasted, 165–66
Lardon Kebabs, Grilled Fig and, 146–48
Lavender Syrup, Navel Oranges with, 222
Leek Salad, Warm, with Oil-Cured Olives and Eggs, 56–58
lemons
    Candied Orange or Lemon Peel, 229–30
    Three Citrus Thick-Cut Marmalade, 227–28
    White Bean Soup with Meyer Lemon, 198
lettuce
    Chicken Braised in White Wine with Peas, 74–75

Fresh Spring Rolls with Thai Dipping Sauce, 66-67
Tomato Aspic with Green Goddess Dressing, 204-6
Lime Pie, California, 220-21

m

main dishes
- Baked Whole Cod with Ginger, Carrots and Green Onions, 77-78
- Barbecued Short Ribs with Dark Sauce, 119-20
- Basic Pasta Recipe, Asian Style, with Sweet Peppers and Tofu (and seasonal variations), 34-35
- Basic Pasta Recipe, Italian Style, with Sautéed Onions and Sweet Red Peppers (and seasonal variations), 32-34
- Basic Savory Tart Recipe with Chard, Spinach, and Bacon (and seasonal variations), 37-40
- Basic Vegetable Fricassee Recipe with Corn and Sweet Pepper (and seasonal variations), 42
- Chicken Braised in White Wine with Peas, 74-75
- Chile Relleno Casserole with Red Sauce, 160-61
- Cracked Dungeness Crab, 211-12
- Creamy Grits with Collard Greens and Wild Mushrooms, 161-63
- Fresh Rag Pasta with Peas and Asparagus, 69-71
- Grilled Eggplant Sandwich with Grilled Sweet Peppers and Basil Aioli, 112-14
- Grilled Fresh Sardines, 107
- Grilled Stuffed Squid, 156-58
- Planked Salmon, 115
- Pork Country Sausage, 158-59
- Pork Rib Roast, Tuscan Style, 217-18
- Roast Chicken with 40 Cloves of Garlic, 109-10
- Roasted Lamb Shanks with Dried Fruits, 165-66
- Savoy Cabbage Rolls Stuffed with Mushrooms and Pork, 213-15
- Sweet Corn and Fresh Oregano Fritters, 102-3
- Tempura Vegetables with Shredded Daikon Dipping Sauce, 207-9
- Young Lamb with Spring Vegetables, 71-72
- Zucchini and Gruyére Gratin, 110-11

Marmalade, Three Citrus Thick-Cut, 227-28
Meringues with Berries, Old-Fashioned, 124-26
Meyer Lemon, White Bean Soup with, 198
Monterey Jack cheese
- Basic Gratin Recipe with Broccoli, 36-37
- Chile Relleno Casserole with Red Sauce, 160-61

mushrooms
- Basic Risotto Recipe with Four Kinds of Mushrooms, 31-32
- Creamy Grits with Collard Greens and Wild Mushrooms, 161-63
- Savoy Cabbage Rolls Stuffed with Mushrooms and Pork, 213-15
- Shiitake Mushroom Soup Shots, 190-91
- Tempura Vegetables with Shredded Daikon Dipping Sauce, 207-9

Musquée de Provence with New Crop Walnuts, 168

n

Navel Oranges with Lavender Syrup, 222
nectarines, *in* Roasted Summer Fruits with Ice Cream, 126

o

Okra with Tomatoes and Onion, Braised, 123
Olives, Oil-Cured, and Eggs, Warm Leek Salad with, 56-58
Olives and Herbs, Roasted Heirloom Tomato Sauce with, 118
onions, green. *See* green and spring onions
Onions, Pickled, 91
oranges
- Candied Orange or Lemon Peel, 229-30
- Navel Oranges with Lavender Syrup, 222
- Radicchio Salad with Blood Oranges, 203
- Three Citrus Thick-Cut Marmalade, 227-28

Oyster Sliders, Fried, with Homemade Tartar Sauce, 195-96

p

pancetta
- Fava Bean Soup with Pancetta, 63
- Frisée Salad with Egg and Pancetta, 152-53
- Grilled Fig and Lardon Kebabs, 146-48
- Homemade Pancetta, 192-94

Parmesan cheese
- Basic Risotto Recipe with Four Kinds of Mushrooms, 31-32
- Devils on Horseback, 189
- Radicchio Salad with Blood Oranges, 203

pasta
- Basic Pasta Recipe, Asian Style, with Sweet Peppers and Tofu (and seasonal variations), 34-35
- Basic Pasta Recipe, Italian Style, with Sautéed Onions and Sweet Red Peppers (and seasonal variations), 32-34
- Fresh Rag Pasta with Peas and Asparagus, 69-71

peaches
- Pickled Peaches, 131-32
- Roasted Summer Fruits with Ice Cream, 126

Pears, Quinces, and Apples, Sautéed, with Whipped Cream, 175
Pears with Blue Cheese, Walnuts, and Honey, 225
peas
- Basic Risotto Recipe with Four Kinds of Mushrooms, 31-32
- Chicken Braised in White Wine with Peas, 74-75
- Fresh Rag Pasta with Peas and Asparagus, 69-71
- Young Lamb with Spring Vegetables, 71-72

peppers, chile
- Chile Relleno Casserole with Red Sauce, 160-61
- Fried Padrón Peppers with Goat Cheese and Crostini, 96

peppers, sweet
- Basic Pasta Recipe, Asian Style, with Sweet Peppers and Tofu, 35
- Basic Pasta Recipe, Italian Style, with Sautéed Onions and Sweet Red Peppers, 33-34
- Basic Vegetable Fricassee Recipe with Corn and Sweet Pepper, 42
- Grilled Eggplant Sandwich with Grilled Sweet Peppers and Basil Aioli, 112-14
- Homemade Ketchup, 133-35

Persimmon Crostini, Grilled, with Farmer Cheese, 144-46
Persimmon Flan, 173-74
pickles. *See* preserved foods
pies and tarts
- Basic Fruit Pie Recipe with Cherries (and seasonal variations), 45-47
- Basic Rustic Sweet Tart Recipe with Apples (and seasonal variations), 43-44
- Basic Savory Tart Recipe with Chard, Spinach, and Bacon (and seasonal variations), 37-40
- California Lime Pie, 220-21
- Old-Fashioned Apricot Pie, 83-85

Pistachios, Fresh Cheese, and Pistachio Oil, Roasted Beet Salad with, 151
Pistachios, Old-Fashioned Butter Cookies with, 176-77
Pistou with Fresh Shelling Beans, Classic Soupe au, 149-50
Planked Salmon, 115
plums
- Plum Jam, 129-30
- Roasted Summer Fruits with Ice Cream, 126

Pluots, *in* Roasted Summer Fruits with Ice Cream, 126
Pomegranate Jelly, 181-82
pork. *See also* bacon; pancetta
- Grilled Stuffed Squid, 156-58

Homemade Pancetta, 192–94
Pork Country Sausage, 158–59
Pork Rib Roast, Tuscan Style, 217–18
Savoy Cabbage Rolls Stuffed with Mushrooms and Pork, 213–15
Wonton Soup with Asian Greens, 200–201

potatoes
Baby Fingerlings with Thyme Blossoms, 79
Basic Roasted Vegetables Recipe with Spring Vegetables, 41
Tempura Vegetables with Shredded Daikon Dipping Sauce, 207–9
Young Lamb with Spring Vegetables, 71–72

preserved foods
Apricot Jam, 89–90
Candied Orange or Lemon Peel, 229–30
Dill Pickles, 139–41
Fall Fruit Chutney, 179–80
Homemade Ketchup, 133–35
Homemade Pancetta, 192–94
Pickled Onions, 91
Pickled Peaches, 131–32
Plum Jam, 129–30
Pomegranate Jelly, 181–82
Pork Country Sausage, 158–59
Roasted Heirloom Tomato Sauce with Olives and Herbs, 118
Summer Tomato Sauce, 136–38
Three Citrus Thick-Cut Marmalade, 227–28
Vin Maison, 92

pumpkin, in Musquée de Provence with New Crop Walnuts, 168

q

Quinces, Apples, and Pears, Sautéed, with Whipped Cream, 175

r

Radicchio Salad with Blood Oranges, 203
Ricotta, Dill, and Smoked Salmon, Bruschetta with, 98
Risotto Recipe with Four Kinds of Mushrooms, Basic (and seasonal variations), 30–32
Roasted Vegetables Recipe with Spring Vegetables, Basic (and seasonal variations), 40–41
Rouille, Old-Fashioned Corn Chowder with, 99–101
Rouille Dipping Sauce, Fried Smelt with, 196
Rustic Sweet Tart Recipe with Apples, Basic (and seasonal variations), 43–44

s

salads
Crab Salad on Belgian Endive Leaves with Avocado, 186
Frisée Salad with Egg and Pancetta, 152–53
Radicchio Salad with Blood Oranges, 203
Roasted Beet Salad with Fresh Cheese, Toasted Pistachios, and Pistachio Oil, 151
Salad of Early Bitter Greens and Late Cherry Tomatoes, 155
Tomato Aspic with Green Goddess Dressing, 204–6
Warm Leek Salad with Oil-Cured Olives and Eggs, 56–58
Watermelon, Cucumber, and Heirloom Cherry Tomato Salad, 104

Salmon, Planked, 115
Salmon, Smoked, Bruschetta with Ricotta, Dill, and, 98
Sardines, Grilled Fresh, 107
sauces and condiments. See preserved foods
Sausage, Pork Country, 158–59

seafood
Baked Whole Cod with Ginger, Carrots and Green Onions, 77–78
Bruschetta with Ricotta, Dill, and Smoked Salmon, 98
Crab Salad on Belgian Endive Leaves with Avocado, 186
Cracked Dungeness Crab, 211–12
Fried Oyster Sliders with Homemade Tartar Sauce, 195–96
Fried Smelt with Rouille Dipping Sauce, 196
Grilled Fresh Sardines, 107
Grilled Stuffed Squid, 156–58
Planked Salmon, 115

seasonal foods
fall, 25, 143
spring, 24, 55
summer, 24–25, 95
winter, 25, 185

seasonal recipe adaptations
fruit pie, 45–47
gratin, 36–37
pasta, 32–35
risotto, 30–32
roasted vegetables, 40–41
rustic sweet tart, 43–44
savory tart, 37–40
vegetable fricassee, 42

Shiitake Mushroom Soup Shots, 190–91
Short Ribs with Dark Sauce, Barbecued, 119–20
side dishes. See also salads
Baby Fingerlings with Thyme Blossoms, 79
Basic Gratin Recipe with Broccoli (and seasonal variations), 36–37
Basic Risotto Recipe with Four Kinds of Mushrooms (and seasonal variations), 30–32
Braised Belgian Endive, 171
Braised Okra with Tomatoes and Onion, 123
Green Garlic Flan, 80–82
Musquée de Provence with New Crop Walnuts, 168
Oven-Roasted Brussels Sprouts with Thyme Butter, 219
Sweet Corn and Fresh Oregano Fritters, 102–3
Tempura Vegetables with Shredded Daikon Dipping Sauce, 207–9

Smelt, Fried, with Rouille Dipping Sauce, 196
Smoked Salmon, Bruschetta with Ricotta, Dill, and, 98

soups
basic stocks, 47–50, 190
Classic Soupe au Pistou with Fresh Shelling Beans, 149–50
Fava Bean Soup with Pancetta, 63
Old-Fashioned Corn Chowder with Rouille, 99–101
Shiitake Mushroom Soup Shots, 190–91
White Bean Soup with Meyer Lemon, 198
Wonton Soup with Asian Greens, 200–201

Spinach, Chard, and Bacon, Basic Savory Tart Recipe with, 38–40

spring
seasonal foods, 24, 55
Apricot Jam, 89–90
Baby Fingerlings with Thyme Blossoms, 79
Baked Whole Cod with Ginger, Carrots and Green Onions, 77–78
Black Cherries in Pinot Noir Gelatin, 86–87
Chicken Braised in White Wine with Peas, 74–75
Deviled Eggs with Tarragon, 59
Fava Bean Soup with Pancetta, 63
Flatbreads with Spring Onions and Feta, 60–62
Fresh Rag Pasta with Peas and Asparagus, 69–71
Fresh Spring Rolls with Thai Dipping Sauce, 66–67
fruit pie variations, 45
Green Garlic Flan, 80–82
Italian Stuffed Artichokes, 64
Old-Fashioned Apricot Pie, 83–85
pasta variations, 33, 34
Pickled Onions, 91
risotto variations, 30
roasted vegetable variations, 40
rustic sweet tart variations, 43
savory gratin variations, 36
savory tart variations, 38
vegetable fricassee variations, 42
Vin Maison, 92
Warm Leek Salad with Oil-Cured Olives and Eggs, 56–58

Young Lamb with Spring Vegetables, 71–72
Spring Onions and Feta, Flatbreads with, 60–62
Spring Rolls, Fresh, with Thai Dipping Sauce, 66–67
Squid, Grilled Stuffed, 156–58
starters. *See* first courses
stocks
    Beef Stock, 49–50
    Chicken Stock, 48–49
    leek and mushroom, 190
    Vegetable Stock, 48–49
stone fruits. *See* specific types
storing foods. *See* preserved foods
summer
    seasonal foods, 24–25, 95
    Barbecued Short Ribs with Dark Sauce, 119–20
    Braised Okra with Tomatoes and Onion, 123
    Bruschetta with Ricotta, Dill, and Smoked Salmon, 98
    Dill Pickles, 139–41
    Fried Padrón Peppers with Goat Cheese and Crostini, 96
    fruit pie variations, 45
    Grilled Eggplant Sandwich with Grilled Sweet Peppers and Basil Aioli, 112–14
    Grilled Fresh Sardines, 107
    Homemade Ketchup, 133–35
    Old-Fashioned Corn Chowder with Rouille, 99–101
    Old-Fashioned Meringues with Berries, 124–26
    pasta variations, 33, 34
    Pickled Peaches, 131–32
    Planked Salmon, 115
    Plum Jam, 129–30
    risotto variations, 30
    Roast Chicken with 40 Cloves of Garlic, 109–10
    Roasted Heirloom Tomato Sauce with Olives and Herbs, 118
    Roasted Summer Fruits with Ice Cream, 126
    roasted vegetable variations, 40
    rustic sweet tart variations, 43
    savory gratin variations, 36
    savory tart variations, 38
    Summer Tomato Sauce, 136–38
    Sweet Corn and Fresh Oregano Fritters, 102–3
    vegetable fricassee variations, 42
    vin maison variation, 92
    Watermelon, Cucumber, and Heirloom Cherry Tomato Salad, 104
    Zucchini and Gruyére Gratin, 110–11
Summer Fruits, Roasted, with Ice Cream, 126
summer squash
    Classic Soupe au Pistou with Fresh Shelling Beans, 149–50
    Zucchini and Gruyére Gratin, 110–11
Summer Tomato Sauce, 136–38

t

Tartar Sauce, Homemade, Fried Oyster Sliders with, 195–96
tarts. *See* pies and tarts
Tempura Vegetables with Shredded Daikon Dipping Sauce, 207–9
Thai Dipping Sauce, Fresh Spring Rolls with, 66–67
Three Citrus Thick-Cut Marmalade, 227–28
tofu
    Basic Pasta Recipe, Asian Style, with Sweet Peppers and Tofu (and seasonal variations), 34–35
    Fresh Spring Rolls with Thai Dipping Sauce, 66–67
tomatoes
    Braised Okra with Tomatoes and Onion, 123
    heirloom, 117
    Homemade Ketchup, 133–35
    Roasted Heirloom Tomato Sauce with Olives and Herbs, 118
    Salad of Early Bitter Greens and Late Cherry Tomatoes, 155
    Summer Tomato Sauce, 136–38
    Tomato Aspic with Green Goddess Dressing, 204–6
    Watermelon, Cucumber, and Heirloom Cherry Tomato Salad, 104
turnips
    Basic Roasted Vegetables Recipe with Spring Vegetables, 41
    Young Lamb with Spring Vegetables, 71–72
Tuscan Style Pork Rib Roast, 217–18

v

Vegetable Fricassee Recipe with Corn and Sweet Pepper (and seasonal variations), 42
Vegetable Stock, 48–49
Vin Maison, 92

w

Walnuts, Blue Cheese, and Honey, Pears with, 225
Walnuts, New Crop, Musquée de Provence with, 168
Watermelon, Cucumber, and Heirloom Cherry Tomato Salad, 104
White Bean Soup with Meyer Lemon, 198
wine
    Black Cherries in Pinot Noir Gelatin, 86–87
    Chicken Braised in White Wine with Peas, 74–75
    Vin Maison, 92
winter
    seasonal foods, 25, 185
    California Lime Pie, 220–21
    Candied Orange or Lemon Peel, 229–30
    Crab Salad on Belgian Endive Leaves with Avocado, 186
    Cracked Dungeness Crab, 211–12
    Devils on Horseback, 189
    Fried Oyster Sliders with Homemade Tartar Sauce, 195–96
    Fried Smelt with Rouille Dipping Sauce, 196
    fruit pie variations, 45
    Homemade Pancetta, 192–94
    Navel Oranges with Lavender Syrup, 222
    Oven-Roasted Brussels Sprouts with Thyme Butter, 219
    pasta variations, 33, 35
    Pears with Blue Cheese, Walnuts, and Honey, 225
    Pork Rib Roast, Tuscan Style, 217–18
    Radicchio Salad with Blood Oranges, 203
    risotto variations, 31
    roasted vegetable variations, 40
    rustic sweet tart variations, 43
    savory gratin variations, 36
    savory tart variations, 38
    Savoy Cabbage Rolls Stuffed with Mushrooms and Pork, 213–15
    Shiitake Mushroom Soup Shots, 190–91
    Tempura Vegetables with Shredded Daikon Dipping Sauce, 207–9
    Three Citrus Thick-Cut Marmalade, 227–28
    Tomato Aspic with Green Goddess Dressing, 204–6
    vegetable fricassee variations, 42
    vin maison variation, 92
    White Bean Soup with Meyer Lemon, 198
    Wonton Soup with Asian Greens, 200–201
Wonton Soup with Asian Greens, 200–201

y

yams, *in* Tempura Vegetables with Shredded Daikon Dipping Sauce, 207–9
Young Lamb with Spring Vegetables, 71–72

z

zucchini
    Classic Soupe au Pistou with Fresh Shelling Beans, 149–50
    Zucchini and Gruyére Gratin, 110–11